The Eight Points Of The Oxford Group

C Irving Benson

269 B47 (2)

THE EIGHT POINTS OF THE
OXFORD GROUP

First Edition - - - 1936
Reprinted - - - - 1936
Reprinted - - - - 1936
Reprinted - - - - 1936
Reprinted - - - - 1937
Reprinted - - - - 1937
Reprinted - - - - 1938

THE EIGHT POINTS OF
THE OXFORD GROUP

AN EXPOSITION FOR
CHRISTIANS AND PAGANS

By

C. IRVING BENSON

HUMPHREY MILFORD
OXFORD UNIVERSITY PRESS
CATHEDRAL BUILDINGS, MELBOURNE
LONDON, EDINBURGH, TORONTO
BOMBAY AND MADRAS
1938

Wholly set up and printed in Australia
by Brown, Prior, Anderson Pty. Ltd.,
Printcraft House, 430 Little Bourke St.,
Melbourne, C.1, 1938.

CONTENTS

IF THIS COUNSEL OR THIS WORK BE
OF MEN, IT WILL BE OVERTHROWN:
BUT IF IT BE OF GOD, YE WILL NOT
BE ABLE TO OVERTHROW THEM; LEST
HAPLY YE BE FOUND EVEN TO BE
FIGHTING AGAINST GOD.

—*GAMALIEL.*

THE CROSS IN LAKELAND

IN all the glory that is England no place has been so chanted by poets and nature lovers as the Lake country in Cumberland and Westmorland—that district which Lowell aptly called 'Wordsworthshire.' Where else in the world is beauty more thickly sown—where is there such unity in variety as in the sweep of landscape which greets the eye from the shores of Coniston or from Kirkstone Pass? Wordsworth, the laureate of Lakeland loveliness, has described the eight valleys seen from the top of Scawfell, diverging like spokes from the nave of a wheel. The scenery of Lakeland is a succession of delightful surprises and of ever changing forms and colours. Rugged mountains rise amid velvety valleys; there is the sparkle of myriad waterfalls and the shimmer of ruffled lakes; glowing foxgloves and other wild flowers in rich profusion bedeck verdant carpets of ferns and lichen-covered rocks are adorned with colours of vivid beauty. Little wonder that such seers as Wordsworth, Southey, Coleridge, De Quincey, Arnold and Ruskin fed their souls in this earthly paradise and littered its winding ways and woodland paths with memories of their presence and poetic thought.

Wordsworth was born in Lakeland. It gave him his cradle, his home and his grave. He loved it with a deep, penetrating, interpreting love. Every tiniest flower was full of deepest suggestion to him. He listened to the music of its running streams, to the song of the skylark and the cuckoo's call, to the whispering leaves and the wind in the trees and caught the deeper accents of a voice divine and saw the Unseen in the seen.

A Spiritual Pilgrimage

On a summer day in the year 1908 there came to this haven of quietness and tranquil beauty a clergyman from Philadelphia, smitten with a sense of failure and futility. He was a Lutheran minister, sick at heart because of the felt lack of the power of God in his life and ministry. A man cannot give what he does not possess and the high calling of the ministry is to give men God. Religion must be infectious; it is, as Dean Inge insists, *caught* rather than *taught*. Of all the wretched men in this world, the most to be pitied is a minister spiritually uncontagious. He may be an eloquent preacher, an efficient organizer, a social success, but if he is a failure in the main issue of his life, he is of all men the most miserable.

This pilgrim, Dr. Frank Buchman, went to Lakeland seeking if haply he might find the secret of the missing power. Not in the many meetings of the Keswick Convention, instinct with spirituality though they were, did he gain that for which he was hungering. Not yet was his heart open and receptive. Then one afternoon he attended a service in a little chapel outside Keswick town and there to a congregation numbering less than twenty an unknown woman, a modern Dinah Morris, told, in simple, artless words, the story of 'Jesus Christ the Crucified.' As she spoke the pilgrim saw the Cross as he had never seen it before and through the Cross he saw himself. That is what the Cross does for us. It throws the searching light of God into the dark places of our hearts and lays bare the things we try to hide even from ourselves. It strips us of the silken robes of self-excusing and tears off the masks wherewith we disguise our condition.

THE LIGHT THAT HURTS

This is the light that hurts and heals. If a man seeks to go on sinning in smug complacency he must contrive to keep out of sight of the Cross— if he can. Frank Buchman remembers little that the nameless preacher said; it was the Word of the Cross he heard. Could there be nobler testimony to a sermon than that? It calls to mind an experience which deeply moved John Henry Jowett. Early one morning he went out from Northfield to conduct in the woods a camp meeting for men drawn from the Jerry McAuley mission for 'down and outers' in New York. Before Jowett spoke one of the men prayed for him: 'Oh, Lord we pray for our brother. Now blot him out! Reveal Thy glory to us in such blazing splendour that he shall be forgotten.' They desired to see 'no man save Jesus only.'

There in the little Cumberland chapel Frank Buchman had a sight of the Cross. Truly, a man may look at a thing nine hundred and ninety-nine times and not see it once, and then look for the thousandth time and see it for the first time. He had resigned his charge after a brush with the trustees. Grudges against these men rankled in his mind. He thought they had been high-handed and hard-hearted in their opposition to him. Resentment was choking his soul, and love, peace and joy cannot abide in a mind rankling with bitterness. With the Cross before his eyes he saw it all. Whatever wrong he had suffered at the hands of others he was not right in himself. There is light in the Cross and there is love—the love that burns to bless. And in the fire of the love of God the sin of pride in this man's heart was burned away.

Thus dawned the creative day in his life. Indeed, life really began for him that day. Thorvalsden, the sculptor, who was born at sea between Iceland and Copenhagen, when questioned as to his birthplace, replied: 'I do not know but I arrived in Rome on March 8, 1797,' dating his real birth from the commencement of his artistic career. Frank Buchman was born in ——. I need not cross the room to make sure. He saw the Cross in 1908.

He walked back exultingly to the house where he was a guest. He had made a great discovery—the greatest discovery that a man ever makes—and he could not keep it to himself. At the tea table he related his experience, simply and quietly but with the contagious gaiety of one who has found what he has long been seeking. Among those who listened to his story was a son of the house, a Cambridge fresher, who suggested a walk after the meal. For hours they walked by Derwentwater, and as they walked, Dr. Buchman told what had happened—how he had seen that to retain his consciousness of God his heart must be empty of all sin and free from the angry past. There by the lake-side that shining youth with a legal mind surrendered his life to Christ.

Dr. Buchman was now a happy man but a self-contained happiness soon evaporates. Next day he sat down and wrote six letters of honest apology to the trustees with whom he had quarrelled, and at the top of each he wrote a verse of the hymn which that lover of Lakeland, Matthew Arnold, regarded as the finest in the English language:

When I survey the wondrous Cross
On which the Prince of Glory died,
My richest gain I count but loss,
And pour contempt on all my pride.

The relief which came to him with this action had a determining effect on his life, for he had learnt that there can be no living and transforming sense of unity with the divine Will, no 'God Consciousness,' so long as the heart nurses bitterness.

CHANGED TO CHANGE

His letters struck no answering chord across the Atlantic; he received no replies, but this silence could not diminish his new-found happiness nor his inward sense of the Divine Presence. That evening walk had brought light to another man and his way was now clearly opening before him. He had been changed; he could be used to change others. This new experience of power working through him led Dr. Buchman to witness to others of the release which had come to him.

Let us pause here for a moment to grasp clearly what had happened to our pilgrim in Lakeland:

1. He had caught a vision of the Cross.
2. He had been convicted of sin in his life.
3. He had made an unreserved surrender to Jesus Christ.
4. He had made frank confession and restitution.
5. He had witnessed to the renewing power of Christ.

From these germinal seeds sprang the principles of his work as a life-changer.

Dr. Buchman returned to America, where, on the recommendation of Dr. John R. Mott, he became what one might call a Chaplain in one of the State Universities. There he had ample opportunity to test the validity of his spiritual experience in meeting the needs of modern youth, and within three years, mainly by personal witness, he had gathered twelve hundred men into his Bible Study Class. Those University years were a period of experiment and preparation for his life work.

Between 1915 and 1919 Dr. Buchman travelled in India and the Far East, all the while growing increasingly sure of the guidance of God. The principles of life changing were gradually formulated in his mind. In the light of what has happened, we can see the guiding hand of Providence in those preparatory years. The very simplicity of the spiritual technique which is meeting the needs of twentieth-century men and women could only have crystallized through brooding quietness and patient waiting. Chesterton apologizes for the length of one of his essays and explains that he had not time to make it shorter. An essay can be written in a hurry—but it takes time to carve an epigram. Not that the principles of life-changing are a cluster of clever epigrams—they are a technique for spiritual power.

One evening a young woman who was a fellow-passenger crossing the Pacific asked Buchman how an ordinary person like herself could change lives for Christ. 'But,' she warned him, 'if you tell me, you must tell me very simply.' That demand was the means of defining in his mind the principles which have formed the basis of the amazing work which he has been able to accomplish.

WORLD CHANGING THROUGH INDIVIDUALS

Again, Dr. Buchman saw clearly that he must apply Christ's own method of changing the world through individuals. In a letter written at this time he set down his conviction as follows: 'This principle (of personalized evangelism) is the essential of Christianity and the absolute essential of all progress. The depersonalization of all

B

activity is one of the great problems of our day. In business, education and in every mission activity we must return to the fundamental principle of Christ as a constant and get into touch with men individually. Those whom we long to win must be in touch with the soul of the movement, which is any human heart aflame with the vital fire.'

Amid all the irreligion, sensualism and reckless abandon of the post-war years, Dr. Buchman felt that the storm troops for a colossal campaign of world changing were to be found in the Universities. Young, athletic, educated, they were for the most part bewildered and nauseated with things as they were, tumbling over one another to get a new sensation, tolerating conventional religion or despising it outright. He knew that no ecclesiastical machinery, no mob missions for youth could capture them for Christ. They wanted neither creed nor argument but they would listen to witness. How to make vital contact with this splendid youth—that was the problem and the opportunity challenging Dr. Buchman. Church services would not answer the purpose—religious meetings were taboo. Some fresh and original way must be found. He attained what he was looking for in the week-end house party, a well-established feature of social life in Britain and America.

THE FIRST HOUSE PARTY

The first house party gathered in Kuling, a summer resort in Central China, where a group of Chinese, British and Americans—missionaries, business men, doctors and politicians spent a fort-night in sharing deeply their experiences, owning up to their failures and then surrendering abso-lutely to Christ to be searched, cleansed, directed and used. In that inaugural party were two Bishops who asked Dr. Buchman to call on their sons in Cambridge when he returned to England.

Thus it came about that in 1921 he visited Cam-bridge, where he captured two undergraduates for Christ. With these he went to Oxford, and in that University also men surrendered to Christ. In the following year a house party was held for men of both Universities and from the number of those who were won to Christ have come many of the leaders in the Group Movement to-day.

One of the men whose life was changed was a Rhodes scholar from South Africa, and he carried the message to his home University. In 1927 a team of six Oxford men and one from Holland visited South Africa. There was a widespread demand for a much larger Group, which was answered in 1929 by the visit of a team of nineteen under Dr. Buchman's leadership. In that land of varied and inflamed nationalisms astonishing things happened. After one Group meeting three hun-dred British and Afrikaans stood and solemnly pledged themselves: 'Sooner shall this limitless veldt pass away, sooner shall this endless sunshine cease, than we Dutch and English-speaking South Africans break the peace which we swear at the feet of Jesus Christ.'

Lives were changed through personal testimony to Jesus Christ by those who had been changed.[1] Recently, an advocate of the Supreme Court declared: 'South Africa without the Oxford Group is unimaginable. There has come a new hope and the promise of racial and class reconciliation on a national scale.'

Three years ago thirty-five men and women went to Canada. and the Prime Minister has said that the influence of the Oxford Group has been felt in every town and village of the Dominion.

Last year, at the invitation of Stortings President, Hambro, an international team of one hundred and fifty visited Norway and in the words of one of her leading editors 'the whole mental outlook of the country has changed.'

The Group has assumed national proportions in Scandinavia and Switzerland. In Switzerland the leaders were received by the President of the Confederation and his Cabinet, and the President of the League of Nations presided over the luncheon which he gave to delegates to the Assembly and members of the Oxford Group International Team. Among those who witnessed at this luncheon in the Hotel Des Bergues were Mr. Louden Hamilton, of Christ Church, Oxford; Brigadier David Forster, of the British Army; Baroness Connie Hahn, of Vienna; the Rt. Hon. C. J. Hambro, President of the Norwegian Parliament; Dr. Frank Buchman; Ma Nyein Tha,

1. The South African press christened them the Oxford Group. The name has stuck and become world-wide.

from Burma; Mr. Bemer Hofmeyr, from South
Africa; Baroness Diana Hahn, of Latvia, and Mr.
James Watt, a former member of the Executive
of the Young Communist League of Great Britain.
After this luncheon a leading delegate to the
Assembly said: 'Unless this message is accepted
there can be no solution of our problems, national
or international.'

A WORLD FORCE

Groups are now in operation in forty-eight
countries stretching from the Arctic Circle to New
Zealand, from Britain to Burma, from the Medi-
terranean to the Far East. The Group entered
Copenhagen in March, 1935. In October twenty-
five thousand Danes assembled in the Forum and
two other halls for a Group Meeting arranged
entirely by their fellow-countrymen—and that
on the very eve of a general election.

This Movement is girdling the globe, lives are
being changed everywhere. And what is its message and method? Nothing more than personal
witness to what Christ is doing for men and women
who have absolutely surrendered their lives to
Him. Not since John Wesley's day has such a
religious movement spread throughout the world.
But what is happening is quite understandable to
those who know the New Testament. It has
jolted us, who regarded ourselves as good church
people, out of our complacency and forced us to
face up to the quality of life set forth in the Book

of Acts. The declared purpose of the Oxford Group is 'a maximum experience of Jesus Christ.'

The world is seething with problems greater than human statesmanship can solve. But there is an answer—there is a solution and we can find it if we will. We must recover the conviction that God has a plan for His world, which was such a passionate belief with the first Christians.

God's plan operating in God's world—that is our objective, and nothing less will meet the needs of our world.

THY WILL BE DONE
ON EARTH AS IN HEAVEN!

DISCOVERY

I cannot invent
   New things,
Like the airships
   Which sail
On silver wings;
   But to-day
A wonderful thought
   In the dawn was given,
And the stripes on my robe,
   Shining from wear,
Were suddenly fair,
   Bright with a light
Falling from Heaven—
   Gold, and silver, and bronze
Lights from the windows of Heaven.
And the thought
   Was this:
That a secret plan
   Is hid in my hand;
That my hand is big,
   Big,
Because of this plan;
That God,
   Who dwells in my hand,
Knows this secret plan
   Of the things He will do for the
     world
Using my hand!
            —Toyohiko Kagawa.

Songs From the Slums (Student Christian Movement).

CHAPTER I

GOD HAS A PLAN FOR EVERY LIFE

SURRENDER

GOD has a plan for the world. But the Divine order can find expression only through our individual lives. The world is made up of individuals—each life a thought of God. This truth was made luminous by one of the speakers at the luncheon in the Hotel Des Bergues, Geneva. Mr. Henry Armistead told the story of a boy sitting in his father's study, at a loose end with nothing to occupy his mind. Weary of doing nothing—the most tiring of all tasks—he asked his father to give him something to do. The father, who was absorbed in his work and irritated at being disturbed, picked up a sheet of paper on which was printed a map of the world, tore it into fragments and threw them on the floor. 'There is a puzzle for you,' he said, 'pick them up and put them together again.' In a surprisingly short time he reassembled the pieces and triumphantly brought the map of the world. 'Well,' said his father, 'you have a better knowledge of geography than I thought.' 'Oh, no,' explained the boy, 'there was a picture of a man on the other side, and I found that when I got the man right, the world came right.' Which things are a parable. Get the individual right and the world will be set right. There is no other way.

1

TELLING THE WORLD

The Oxford Group is telling the world what Christians have always theoretically believed—that God has a plan for every man and woman and that no life need walk with aimless feet. That plan can be definitely known if we fulfil God's conditions.

What would be thought of a builder who went on constructing a house without reference to the architect's plan? There is as surely a design plotted out for each one of us as ever there was for Abraham, Joseph, David or St. Paul. The weavers of tapestries rejoiced when they had a genius like Raphael[1] to paint picture patterns for their weaving. What a discovery for us to make that there is a plan for our lives made by the Eternal Wisdom who 'seeth the end from the beginning!' For lack of this knowledge millions of men and women are mentally sick, blasé, disgusted with themselves and the world at large. If life has no meaning it is not worth living.

There is a story of a man who was waiting on a platform for his train and was struck by the wretched appearance of a dog tied to a post. He called the porter, and said: 'That dog looks miserable. Where is it going to?' 'That's the trouble,' said the porter. 'I don't know, and you don't know, and the dog don't know. He's chewed up his label.' How many people are like that, miserable because they have lost all sense of

1. Several of Raphael's cartoons for tapestry weavers are in the British Museum.

direction in life. They don't know where they are going. The sense of futility is slowly destroying them.

The greatest of human miseries, the most deadly disease, is not cancer but boredom. There is more wretchedness, more torment driving men to folly due to boredom than to anything else. To all the disappointed, disillusioned, weary children of men the Oxford Group proclaims in the name of Christ: 'God has a plan for our lives and the real adventure of being alive is to find it and achieve it.' Well did Woodrow Wilson say that, when you have settled what is the chief end in life, you have settled everything else. It is better to have something to live for than to have much to live on.

One of the noblest sermons in the English language is that of the American saint, Dr. Horace Bushnell, entitled, 'Every Man's Life a Plan of God.' It is not mere preaching but the witness of a great man's personal experience. Here is the heart of it:

'What do the Scriptures shew us, but that God has a particular care for every man, a personal interest in him, and a sympathy with him and his trials, watching for the uses of his one talent as attentively and kindly, and approving him as heartily, in the right employment of it, as if He had given him ten; and what is the giving out of the talent itself, but an exhibition of the fact that God has a definite purpose, charge, and work, be it this or that, for every man! . . .

'*There is a definite and proper end, or issue, for every man's existence; an end which, to the heart of God, is the good intended for him, or for which he was intended; that which he is privileged to become, called to become, ought to become; that which God will assist him to become, and which he cannot miss, save by his own fault. Every human soul has a complete and perfect plan cherished for it in the heart of God—a divine biography marked out, which it enters into life to live. . . .*

'*But there is, I must add, a single but very important and even fearful qualification. Things all serve their uses, and never break out of their place. They have no power to do it. Not so with us. We are able, as free beings, to refuse the place and the duties God appoints; which, if we do, then we sink into something lower and less worthy of us. . . .*'

LIFE A DISCOVERY

'*How inspiring and magnificent to live, by holy consent, a life all discovery; to see it unfolding, moment by moment, a plan of God, our own life-plan conceived in His paternal love; each event, incident, experience, whether bright or dark, having its mission from Him, and revealing, either now or in its future issues, the magnificence of His favouring counsel; to be sure, in the dark day, of a light that will follow, that loss will terminate in gain, that trial will issue in rest, doubt in satisfaction, suffering in patience, patience in purity, and all in a consummation of greatness and dignity that even God will look on with a smile! How magnificent, how strong in its repose, how full of rest is such a kind of life!'*

Yes! but to read all this avails nothing unless we can prove it for ourselves. Is there a technique of finding one's life plan? There is. The initial step and the indispensable step in the quest is: ABSOLUTE SURRENDER OF OUR LIVES TO GOD. Surrender is 'life under new management.'

Surrender is not something to be done once and for all at the start, but a process to be sustained, alike in mood and in action, all the way through. Indeed, it must be more than sustained; it must be continuously deepened and informed. Every new day must be surrendered to God. The only surrender that has value is the surrender of life in its totality. Anything consciously kept back mars everything. All that is in self, good, bad and indifferent, must be handed over to God. He will then give back whatever is fit for us to use.

It may reasonably be asked how it is possible to surrender the bad self. If an evil habit, for instance, can be exorcised by mere surrender, it would then seem that we can save ourselves. But can we? No! for the surrender is made possible by the operation of the Holy Spirit within us so that while we play our own part in it, we can in no case suppose that we are saving ourselves.

Darling Virtues

A man asks why he should be required to surrender what is obviously good in his life. For
example, there is his love of his child, and, surely,
it was never intended that he should surrender
that. But it is intended so, for a father can do
nothing better, either for himself or for his child,
than to yield his natural affection, good as it is, to
Christ. If we do not trust Christ with undisputed
use of all that is already pure and true in human
life, we do not trust Him at all. Christ makes
a difference even to what is naturally good in our
lives. We speak of darling sins which keep men
out of the Kingdom, but there are darling virtues
which may keep them out just as effectively. The
man who was 'not far from the Kingdom of God'
was yet not in it. This may seem hard doctrine,
but it is the inescapable demand of Christ. Any
man who would follow Christ must surrender to
Him all that he is and has—the whole man and
his outfit. Christ claims all. He asks no more
and He will take no less. Hudson Taylor used
to say: 'If you don't crown Him Lord of all
you don't crown Him Lord at all.'

The man who asks what is the least he can give
up in order to be a Christian has not even begun
to see what surrender means. Christianity is an
uncalculating mood; for when a man has counted
the cost and resolved to meet it, he has done with
the prudential and bargaining spirit.

Surrender is bound to be shallow and frag-
mentary where it is not accompanied by repentance.

Until a man knows himself to be a sinner, he is unaware of the real tragedy of his life and unable to make an intelligent surrender. Repentance is the very breath of surrender. And this is the first thing the Cross does for us as it did for a man in Lakeland. In the searching sight of Christ we see sin not as a transgression of law, not as rebellion against light; but as a blow struck at love. It is not so much our concern as to what Christ will do to us but what we have done and are doing to Him. I used to be afraid that God might hurt me; but when I saw the Cross I saw how I had hurt God who wills me good and not evil.

Repentance requires a recognition of the facts about ourselves. 'Not carefully manufactured self-depreciation, but sincerity with ourselves is the true condition of penitence,' says Dr. John Oman. The capacity of the human mind for self-deception is unlimited. The Cross enables us to be sincere with ourselves—it is the one place in life where we cannot play the hypocrite.

The trouble with us is not a list of wrongs that can be added up but the general state of wrongness. We may point to this or that in our lives and say that we will have done with it and doubtless we mean it. But we soon begin to find that our lives are not made up of separate pieces that can be separately mended. Life is of one piece. If we make no radical change except to mend some particular fault we find ourselves giving way to it again because of some weakness at another point. It is the whole of life that must be turned and changed.

A New Way of Looking at Things

Bishop Westcott maintained that repentance is an entire revolution of our view of God, ourselves and the world. Repentance is really a change of mind. It is not only a change of thinking but a change of the thing with which we think. 'Repent!' said Jesus. Change the character of your mind! Get a new way of looking at things. Literally—think the other way. To repent is to substitute Christ's viewpoint in place of our own. It means a complete revaluation of all things including those which we are inclined to think good.

Repentance is more than fickle regret. Tears may be as cheap as raindrops or they may be as costly as pearls. Again, it is more than remorse, which is only self-accusation and self-loathing, issuing in despair. Remorse may become destructive morbidity. Regret which remains only regret is useless. Repentance is unto life. It is vital to effective living. Repent and live!

Change of mind—a new way of looking at things—reveals to us that we belong to God and must therefore absolutely surrender ourselves and be entirely at His disposal. The surrender of self must include every interest, possession and relationship. If self is kept back from God, life will be a series of reluctances and irritations. And that is often the trouble. We try to be religious in patches while the great surrender has not been made. These smaller surrenders encounter curbs and restraints and the soul is irritated and divided against itself. Until we surrender, praying and waiting will avail nothing. We shall be disappointed and we must expect to be.

Are we willing to make a full surrender? to yield ourselves absolutely to God? That is the great question. What God wants is not praising lips, nor reverence and prayers only—but ourselves, our powers and capacities and possessions— not a tenth of our income and one-seventh of our time, but all our income and all our time. And He will show us—give us guidance—as to what He wants us to spend upon ourselves and in the extension of His Kingdom. The clear ringing challenge of the Oxford Group Movement is this: are you willing to let God run your life, or will you keep it in your own hands? Are you wanting to use God for your purposes or are you willing to let Him use you for His purposes? How much of prayer is an attempt to induce God to further our wishes instead of lifting our wishes into the range of His will!

The Group takes the uncompromising line that every Christian ought to be a life-changer and that the thing that keeps the nominal Christian from being the force which he ought to be is the presence of sin in his own life, and nothing else. 'Sin,' says Frank Buchman, 'is anything that keeps one from God or from another person.' Sin is whatever unfits us to do God's will.

c

The Sin of Compromise

The most common sin among us is compromise. Our state is one of half-surrender. Our service is largely self-effort, self-chosen and self-directed. We have particular sins which we want God to deal with, but others which we propose to reserve to ourselves. *Punch* has a story of a little boy who got his prayer muddled and said: 'Let my friends be all forgiven. Bless the sins I love so well.' Our pet sins keep us from God. That is why He isn't real to us and why we are unhappy and so pathetically useless. Until the last sin has been bared to God for surgical treatment there can be no real victory in our lives. A young man in one of the Groups said that at first he wanted to 'hand-pick his sins,' giving over to God what he wanted to be rid of but keeping certain comfortable indulgences for himself.

When the Saxons were baptized in the time of Charlemagne they insisted upon keeping their right arms above the water. They were willing to consecrate 'all except' their fighting arms. How that incomplete surrender explains much that is thwarting God's plan for the world to-day!

If we wholly surrender ourselves to God, that is, bring our wills into agreement with God's will, God will work through us for the salvation and right development of humanity and the perfection of its environment. Of this there is no doubt. How then can we look out on the world with its war and unemployment, greed and selfishness, without being convicted? Our unsurrendered lives have denied God the use of us in changing the world. Are we not responsible to God for the condition of the world to-day? How can we have a better world? Where shall we begin? Plainly, with the surrender of our own lives. And, when we become life-changers all, it will surprise us to see how a movement spreads and captures the imagination of nations once it wins its way.

Well did Austin Dobson pray:

'Make this thing plain to us, O Lord!
    That not the triumph of the sword—
Not that alone—can end the strife,
    But reformation of the life—
But full submission to Thy word!
    Not all the stream of blood outpoured
Can peace—the long desired—afford;
    Not tears of mother, maid or wife—
Make this thing plain!
'We must root out our sins ignored,
    By whatsoever name adored:
Our secret sins, that, ever rife,
    Shrink from the operating knife,
Then shall we rise, renewed, restored—
    Make this thing plain!'

Despite the ardent longing for peace on earth and the utter disgust with war, peace will never be established so long as our lives are poisoned by hatreds, jealousies, resentments and greed—the very things, which, multiplied by millions, make wars.

How God Works

God has entrusted us with the risky gift of freedom, the power to choose our own way, thus limiting Himself to the extent of respecting our personalities. The way God works in the world without destroying our freedom is through our personalities. He does not hang miracles upon nothing—He is ever watching and waiting for men and women whom He can use as instruments —no, as something more than instruments,—as fellow-workers. The best answer I know to the question, ' Why are we here? ' is that of St. Paul: ' We are God's fellow-workers.' What light and leading, what power and peace are denied to the whole human family because we are not co-operating with God!

A new world order—the Divine order—can come only through surrendered lives. The creative experience in the life of Dwight L. Moody, the founder of Northfield, was when he heard a lay preacher say: ' The world has yet to see what God will do with, and for, and through, and in, and by, a man who is fully and wholly consecrated to Him.' ' He said "a man," ' soliloquized Moody. ' He did not say a great man, nor a learned man, nor a rich man, nor a wise man, nor an eloquent man, nor a " smart " man, but simply "a man." I am a man, and it lies with the man himself whether he will, or will not, make that entire and full consecration. I will try my utmost to be that man.' And Dwight L. Moody became one of the most successful life-changers of the nineteenth century.

It is wonderful what God can do with even a broken life—if He is given all the pieces! Surrender has to be inclusive rather than exclusive. We have suffered from a religion of mutilation. If I become a Christian must I give up dancing, theatres, smoking, sport? The answer is that we must surrender everything to God and then receive back from His hands whatever He gives and use it for His Kingdom. George Muller tells us how we may check whether we are entirely surrendered. 'In everything you do ask yourself this question: "Why do I do this?" and if the answer is always every time, "For the glory of God," you are entirely consecrated.'

Your Money and Your Life

Christianity surely means the consecration of the whole life—work, pleasure, money, everything. The highwaymen of olden time used to hold up their victims and demand 'your money *or* your life.' Christ demands our money *and* our lives. Christianity means devotion to a Person—issuing in a new spirit, a new purpose, and a new programme.

The Christian life is not narrow and sickly and impoverished—it is a rich, ample, radiant life. It is not a fumbling, crippled, dingy existence, full of suppressions and prohibitions and exclusions, but a life of buoyant virility and disciplined action. It certainly rejects 'anything that defileth' or 'worketh abomination or maketh a lie.' But all that is clean and joyous and wise and beautiful may be

welcomed and brought under the sway of the Kingdom. Christ does not want to silence our music and
kill our poetry and deaden our imagination; for He
is not to be the ruler of a mere corner of our life.
Everything must come under His rule. Christianity does not call us to a timid acquiescence in a
chilling, bloodless, passionless existence—it sum-
mons us to great adventure, to stern conflict, to
glorious service.

The temptation to Church people—so subtle
that it may quite escape notice, yet so insidious that
it may be mastering us all the while—is that of
being content, after a beginning made in enthusi-
astic fervour, with a victory half-won. The
Christian above all others needs to remember the
searching truth—stern and awful in its implications
—that the good may be the enemy of the best.
The Christian man is so far from the worst that he
may fail to realize how far he is from the best.

SURRENDERING THE LAST SECRET

That maximum Christian, Dr. F. B. Meyer,
shared this intimate experience. He was, he confessed, a minister in a Midland town in England,
not at all happy, doing his work for the pay he got
and holding a good position amongst his fellows.
Hudson Taylor and two young students came into
his life. He watched them. They had something
that he had not. Those young men stood before
him in all their strength and joy. One of the
students was Charles Studd, a Cambridge Blue
and a Test cricketer.

'What is the difference,' asked Meyer, 'between you and me? You seem so happy, and I somehow am in the trough of the wave.' Studd replied: 'There is nothing that I have which you may not have.'

'But how am I to get it?'

'Well,' he said, 'have you given yourself right up to God?'

'I winced,' said Dr. Meyer, 'I knew that, if it came to that, there was a point where I had been fighting my deepest convictions for months. . . . I thought I would do something with Christ that night which would settle it one way or the other, and I met Christ. . . . I knelt in my room and gave Christ the keys of my will with the exception of the key of a cupboard in one back storey in my heart. He said to me:

'"Are they all here?"

'And I said: "All but one."

'"What is that?" He asked.

'"It is the key of a little cupboard," said I, "in which I have got something with which Thou needest not interfere, for it is mine."

'Then, as He put the keys back into my hand, and seemed to be gliding away to the door, He said:

'"My child, if you cannot trust Me with all, you do not trust Me at all."'

There and then Dr. Meyer yielded the last key of the last secret and his life became like a mill-race of Divine power.

GOOD, THE ENEMY OF THE BEST

How the good may easily become the enemy of the best was set in startling light when Christ said: 'Verily I say unto you, that the publicans and the harlots go into the Kingdom of God before you.' The little religion we have may be an illicit shelter, a means of evading the realism of Christ's demands.

He told a story of two men, the one a Pharisee and the other a publican, who went up to the Temple to pray. In the eyes of their fellows, the Pharisee was the saint, the publican the sinner. But Jesus turned the world's verdict upside down: 'This man,' He said—the publican, not the Pharisee, the sinner, not the saint—'went down to his house justified'—accepted of God—rather than the other.

Again—'Whosoever hateth his brother is a murderer.' One man, in a frenzy of sudden passion, when the blood in his veins is running liquid fire, smites and slays a fellow-man, and his crime lands him in the murderer's dock. Another shoots the viewless shafts of his malice and hate. But if Jesus is right, whose is the greater sin?

THE SHEWING UP OF SIN

There is—to use one of Kipling's phrases—'a damnable streak' in most of us that always leads us to listen for the man in the next pew. That is the trouble with so much of our sermon-hearing. Even in Church we put up the ample umbrella of self-complacency, and all the rain of Christ's condemnation—His condemnation of our sins—runs off on to the shoulders of our neighbours.

Nor can it be forgotten that it was a group of religious people, priests and Pharisees, who sent Christ to the Cross. They did not want to be disturbed, but to be left alone in the snugness of their half-faith. They were respectable citizens, regular churchgoers. Read the story again. It is all so human, all so understandable. Now the Cross shows us to ourselves, exposes our excuses, unmasks our motives. This is what private sins in religious people are capable of—murdering the very Son of God. The Cross makes us see the desperate nature of sin. Behind the tragedy of Calvary are the ordinary lives of men and women to whom little sins seemed harmless until at last they tried to murder God. The Cross gives the truth a chance to operate on our consciences. To see sin in the light of the Cross is to see that there is not a thing on earth worth sinning for.

CHAPTER II

CONFESSION IS GOOD FOR THE SOUL

Sharing

WE have seen how Dr. Frank Buchman learned the value of 'sharing' when, on that memorable day, he opened his mind to the Cambridge fresher as they walked the lake side together. He was greatly helped by the unburdening of his soul and so was his companion. What he did was to rediscover the value of the spiritual prescription which St. James gave in his Epistle, 'Confess your faults one to another, and pray one for another that ye may be healed.'[1] Dr. Buchman prefers the more familiar word 'sharing' instead of confession, but the experience is the same.

Again and again we have said that 'Confession is good for the soul,' but have we ever paused to realize the vital truth contained in that easy platitude? Confession is not only good for the soul, but is essential for the soul. There is continuous and widespread testimony to the value of St. James's advice, but there are thousands of men and women whose lives will never be clean, confident and effective until they have bravely confessed their sins.

A story is told that round the gates of heaven hangs an uneasy crowd of five or six hundred people. They all come from one English village,

1. St. James 5: 16.

and the gatekeeper has orders to let them all in at
once if any one of them will admit that he or she
ever made a mistake. Not one of them, however,
will 'lower himself' so far before the rest, so there
they all are and are likely to remain. Is it not true
that crowds of people keep themselves outside the
Kingdom of God with all its wonderful forgiveness, peace and joy, because some poisonous pride
or silly fear prevents them finding release by confession of their sins? Unless we are prepared to
give ourselves away, we shall soon find that in the
service of God we have very little to give.

The value of confession has been spoiled for
many of us, by enforcing it when it should be spontaneous and by allowing it to become a substitute
for real penitence and life changing. But we must
not permit any prejudice to offend us or to make us
unwilling to examine the plain teaching of the New
Testament regarding confession.

BEING OPEN

The counsel given by St. James is evidence that
mutual confession was practised in the early Christian groups. The practice, however, fell into such
sad abuse that the Reformation abolished it. In the
eighteenth century, Wesley had the wisdom to see
that the Reformers in their zeal had thrown away
some valuable customs of the early Church and
he bravely recovered them. Among the practices he
revived was confession. He instituted 'bands' or
groups for those who were seeking a maximum
experience of Christ. Wesley laid great stress on

what he called, being 'open.' At every meeting members asked each other: (1) 'What known sins have you committed since our last meeting?' (2) 'What temptations have you met with?' (3) 'How were you delivered?' (4) 'What have you thought, said or done of which you doubt whether it be sin or not?'

Once a week the united bands held a meeting for Christian witness. Wesley regarded those who met in these bands as the vanguard of Methodism. It is no small loss to the effectiveness of Methodist discipline and spiritual efficiency that these bands gradually died out.

The Oxford Group Movement has rendered inestimable service to the Church in rediscovering the importance of confession. By open confession groups of men and women have gained victory in their lives and a new sense of spiritual fitness and gladness. The Group insists on the power of sharing to fill the spirit with an entirely new sense of life. And this is not at all mysterious. Sharing comes of a willingness to be absolutely honest about oneself; it is a sign that the long attempt to compromise is over, an indication that the personality is no longer divided within itself, an evidence that the soul really means what it says. Directly we are honest with God, with ourselves and with other people, we are born again. There cannot be any vital experience of religion while selfishness remains, whatever form it takes. All selfishness is sin and all sin is a form of selfishness. It is surprising that so many good people can go on deceiving themselves—men and women who are moral and generous but with some root of selfishness in their hearts which prevents them from experiencing a vital religion and being life changers.

'Confess therefore your sins one to another that ye may be healed.' St. James did not say, 'Confess your sins to God only.' We must confess to God —we must begin with Him—'Against Thee and Thee only have I sinned.' Sharing is not a substitute for confession to God who alone can forgive. But as a matter of experience it is a relatively uncostly thing to fall on our knees and confess our sins to God in secret. We may glibly repeat the General Confession: 'We have done those things which we ought not to have done and we have left undone those which we ought to have done, and there is no health in us.' That is a terrible thing to say—'There is no health in us,' but it is most terrible of all when we do not keenly feel how terrible it is, as though we had never heard of victory over sin. It is not difficult to confess to sin in general, for then we do not confess any sin in particular. It is very costly, however, to say these things in the presence even of an entirely loving human being whom we can trust but as a matter of experience it is extraordinarily effective in putting the knife to our sins. Almost every vital movement in Christian history has made some use of this practice.

SHARING MAKES FORGIVENESS REAL

We cannot feel the reality of forgiveness until we have confessed. To very many people God is unreal. It is so hard for them to realize that He is present and to tell them to confess to God alone is to deprive them of the relief and sense of reality which sharing confers. Their solitary search for forgiveness is generally unsuccessful. The forgiveness of God is an amazing gift but it is hard to believe and accept the gift. Sharing makes God's pardon real. Peace without forgiveness is impossible and confession is the way to forgiveness and therefore the way to peace. Forgiveness does not depend upon confession but its appropriation does.

St. James certainly did *not* say, 'Confess other people's sins.' There is always hope for a man when he confesses his sins. It is the man who confesses other men's sins for whom it is difficult to hope. When Moody visited St. Andrew's, the whole community was stirred from the lowest to the highest. Dr. A. K. H. Boyd wittily summed up the results of the campaign by saying that even two Principals had been confessing their sins—Principal Tulloch confessing the sins of Principal Shairp and Principal Shairp confessing the sins of Principal Tulloch! That is a way we have and very frequently the sins we confess for others are the very sins we hide in our own hearts. Shakespeare makes Timon of Athens ask. 'Wilt thou whip thine own faults in other men?' This is what the psychologists call compensation—the condemning in others of what we refuse to admit in our-

selves. Paul told the Romans: 'Therefore thou
art inexcusable, O man, whosoever thou art that
judgest, for wherein thou judgest another thou
condemnest thyself: for thou that judgest doest
the same things.' The power of self-deception is
terrible and we need to be absolutely honest with
ourselves lest the light in us be darkened.

The emancipating effect of sharing, or mutual
confession, is universally admitted by psychologists. We say: 'Get it off your chest and you'll
feel better.' Confession is the pouring out from
the soul of all its repressed and hidden sins, together with its burdens, griefs and sorrows. To
throw them off is necessary for spiritual health, for
unless sin is confessed, it produces a brooding and
depression which paralyze effort and slay hope.
Many who yearn to live good lives are held up by
some unacknowledged sin, which festers within.

There they are—those hidden sins—fraud, the
burden of lives, thefts, treachery, slander, impurity
and the subtle duplicity of conflicting ideals. There
they are like subterranean fires, periodically breaking out in fits of depression, weeping, temper or
in physical breakdown.

The open acknowledgment of weaknesses and
sins has a remarkably liberating effect in most cases
of troubled conscience, despondency over failure,
fear of human opinions and the like. When a timid
seeker after God breaks through the inhibitions of
moral cowardice, there comes an inrush of divine
life and light and he becomes conscious of being
possessed and guided by a power not his own—the
power of the Holy Spirit.

THE INSTINCT TO CONFESS

We must not forget that James was speaking of sickness and he recommended confession as a real part of the healing. A man would be far more likely to benefit by medical treatment and prayers for healing if he unburdened his soul and cleared up differences between himself and other people. Many a life would tingle with health and gladness by obeying this injunction of St. James. We wear out our hearts in estrangements and friction is created by our native stubbornness in defending a fault rather than confess it. Far be it from me to suggest that all nervous storms and breakdowns are due to sin; but every psychologist testifies to the fact that many of them are. Dr. Schofield, a Harley Street nerve specialist, has said: 'I believe that many go mad, more relapse into melancholia, and multitudes get confirmed in evils of all sorts, for want of an outlet to their hidden thoughts and troubles. . . . I am convinced by long experience, that a man who did nothing else but listen with interest and kindness to the troubles of broken hearts would thereby do much good and relieve much suffering.'

Confession is an instinct of the soul. As sin is the symptom of spiritual sickness, so confession is the appointed means for the recovery of health. The story of the heart of Robert Burns—the un-uttered sob in the poet's soul—is an example of how tragic life may become for want of sharing. Burns lamented that he could not pour out his inmost soul without reserve to any human being.

He commenced a journal of his own mental history 'as a substitute,' he said, 'for a confidential friend.' He felt that he must have 'something' in which he could unbosom himself, 'without peril of having his confidence betrayed.' We all need someone with whom we can be perfectly frank.

Then consider the story of Lucy Snowe as related by Charlotte Brontë who was probably weaving from her autobiography when she wrote the confessional scene in *Vilette*. Lucy was a poor English governess in Belgium, left alone in school during the long vacation. One evening she heard the church bells. Sick and lonely at heart she strayed into church and almost mechanically entering the confessional box poured out her distress into the ear of an old French priest. Instead of commencing with the usual prelude she said: 'Mon Pere, Je suis Protestante!' He inquired, not unkindly, why, being a Protestant, she came to him. She told him that she was perishing for a word of advice and comfort. She had been living alone for weeks, had been ill, and was sorely depressed in mind; indeed, she could no longer endure the strain. But she was out of the old priest's depth. He knew only the routine work. 'You take me unawares,' he said, 'I have not had such a case as yours. . . . Go, my daughter, but return again to me.' She had not expected more. But the mere act of telling her troubles gave her relief. She was already solaced and returned to the priest no more.

D

What is Lucy Snowe—a Protestant in a Belgian Confessional—but a witness to the heart's instinctive cry to confess, to unburden itself? Our natural reticence, however, and our desire for the good opinion of others, make us shrink from taking a course apparently so opposed to proper self-respect. 'What will be thought of me,' we argue, 'if I confess to such internal rottenness?' We are all in desperate need of forgiveness; but we do not receive it because we are insanely anxious to keep up a good appearance. Our reluctance to confess is as marked as our longing for it. And this holding back takes some strange forms. The more resentful a man is at the suggestion that it is necessary, the more likely it is that his own conscience is nettling him. Probably the greatest hindrance is fear of betrayal. So confession is not made and the transgression remains unforgiven.

THE GROUP GIVES FRIENDLY CONTACTS

Now the experience of the Group is totally different. If others have not committed the same deeds, they have been guilty of others just as bad. There is not much to pick and choose among sins except that the sins of the spirit are even more stubborn than the sins of the flesh as Jesus showed. In the friendly contacts which the Group offers, mutual confidence is engendered and an atmosphere created in which specific and definite confession can be mutually made. The sense of relief is immediate. The soul, 'disburdened of her load,' as Wesley sings, rises exultant. The way is cleared for the inrush of Divine energy and there springs up a buoyancy of spirit, a sense of freedom and of power which makes witness natural and spontaneous, and life-changing a congenial and even necessary field for self-expression. It is wonderful to be simple and sincere, and the joy of it is so profound, that those in the Group voluntarily confess what an Inquisition could not have dragged from them. Many people long hindered by a sense of guilt have had the stain of guilt removed through sharing, and so have been liberated to live freer and happier lives. Others, whose lives have been maimed by a haunting memory of some unworthy experience, have found marvellous relief through sharing.

No part of the Oxford Group Movement has been so severely criticized, and so wildly misrepresented as sharing. That there are dangers no one need deny. But then all living things are dangerous. Only dead things are safe. Public sharing *is* dangerous. Even surrendered people put frills on an experience if they tell it often. Repetition robs it of spontaneity and reality. Public confession of disreputable sins may lead to the moral sin of spiritual pride. Such confession may degenerate into prurient exhibitionism. To rehearse one's past sins may give the same gratification as the actual commission of the sins, only without a sense of guilt. Again, it may give to the individual a sense of importance which he or she has never before been able to achieve. The Groups themselves are more alive to these perils than their

CHAPTER III

IF THY BROTHER HATH AUGHT AGAINST THEE—

RESTITUTION

WE have made so much, though not enough, of Christ reconciling man to God that we have not sufficiently grasped His gospel of reconciliation between man and man. Let a man be right with God, and the love of man will inevitably follow—so we should say.

But Christ takes pains to state the contrary. 'Therefore, if thou bring thy gift to the altar, and there rememberest that thy brother hath aught against thee; Leave there thy gift before the altar, and go thy way; first be reconciled to thy brother, and then come and offer thy gift.'[1] He vividly pictures for us a worshipper before the very altar. There in the silence, out of the hallowed hush comes a voice saying solemnly and searchingly, 'Has thy brother aught against thee?' While the priest is in the very act of offering his sacrifice, a sudden flash of awakened memory shows him a brother man who is offended. The solemn sacrifice is interrupted while he seeks the offended brother

---

1. Matt. 5: 23, 24. 'So if you remember, even when offering your gift at the altar, that your brother has any grievance against you, leave your gift at the very altar and go away; first be reconciled to your brother, then come back and offer your gift' (Moffatt).

30

and makes up the quarrel; then he comes back and takes up the interrupted worship. Such a strange and startling action was a breach of liturgical propriety. Yet that, our Lord teaches, is better than the blight of an unforgiving spirit. We cannot make effective contact with God, we cannot truly worship while our hearts are choked with resentments.

Jesus denounces ritual only when it becomes a refuge from the ethical demands of His teaching. Coming to the altar is good, for it awakens memory, but it will be futile unless we act immediately upon the revelation which comes to us. True worship enables us to test our conduct by God's will for us and for others. It redeems from blindness, listlessness and self-concern, and gives us new insight into our obligations to God's other children. When it fails to do this, our worship is ineffective. We are told to leave the altar when we know we have offended anyone and seek his forgiveness. Jesus insists that the altar must be related to life and that His teaching shall dominate our community relationships. Our task to-day is to look at the Sermon on the Mount not as the wild dream of a Galilean visionary, but as a piece of realism—the only plan upon which men can live together in peace and security.

THE CHRISTIAN INITIATIVE

We are all human, liable to give and take offence so that love is soured with hatred and goodwill cools off and freezes into icy indifference. Misunderstandings do and will arise and estrangements are bound to happen. In a world like this, being what we are, it is impossible but that offences should come. But because anger is such a destructive thing Jesus points out the urgency of reconciliation and restitution. So urgent is it that a man had better leave even the worship of God to right any wrong. Jesus does not suggest that Christians will not fall out; but the test of their Christianity is how quickly they seek to make up the quarrel. 'It takes two to make a quarrel, but one can always end it.' The Christian must take the initiative. 'A more glorious victory cannot be gained over another man than this, that while the injury began on his part the kindness should begin on ours,' said Tillotson.

Jesus saw that one of the most prolific sources of human misery lies in the spirit that harbours grudges for wrongs inflicted. So He taught forgiveness, not as a luxury, but as an inescapable necessity. He bids us 'agree with thine adversary quickly'—*quickly*, so that enmity will not have time to grow. Settle your differences before you separate, or a difference becomes a hatred and a hatred a passion for revenge. Nurse a grievance and it grows like Jack's beanstalk. Half a day's steady thinking upon some slight makes it appear one of the greatest crimes in the history of a century. Once we have formed the habit of nursing grievances we shall never lack one to nurse. There will always be someone to injure us, sting us and betray us.

St. Paul, who stands next to Jesus in his clear insight into human nature, and who read men like open books, warned us, 'Be not overcome with evil but overcome evil with good.' Of course, the other party is to blame—Paul assumes that, but our just resentment may become a longing for revenge and satisfaction which opens the gate to a flood of unrestrained passion. Jesus went beyond the old law: '*I* say unto you forgive your enemies.' It is the only practical solution. No other method works.

Vindictiveness does not succeed. It cannot succeed. Trying to cure evil with evil is as futile as trying to put out a fire with kerosene. Any passing zip of false delight that we experience in 'getting even' is soon eaten up by the fierce acids generated by an unsympathetic outlook.

Anger is a waste of nerve force, vitality, and spiritual life. If we allow things to rankle, they poison our minds, disturb our sleep and pauperize our lives.

THE CHRISTIAN STRATEGY

Without forgetfulness and forgiveness life is choked and poisoned by memories and antipathies. We lose the very qualities that make us human. The world is well-nigh exhausted trying to settle personal, political, industrial and international complications by an iron system of justice which is little better than legalized revenge. If this were the only way the outlook for men and nations would be hopeless. But there is a better and more effective method, and it is this: 'Overcome evil with good.' This is the Christian strategy. Truly there is time and place for righteous anger against wrong, but how easily it becomes clouded with the smoke of personal vindictiveness! Two wrongs do not make a right—they are incapable of ever doing so. Distressing things happen to most of us— venomous attacks which seem hardly explicable save on the theory that everybody is mad at some point. Forgiveness is not easy. A deep personal wrong wounds and stings. But for our own sakes we must not harbour thoughts of revenge. If we are the injured party we must take the initiative because we are in the stronger position. Our innocence is our strength. The supreme example of the wronged taking the initiative is the Cross. 'While we were yet sinners Christ died for us—the just for the unjust.' He forgave the very men who drove the nails through His hands and feet.

'Cut your losses,' said Jesus, 'and make it up somehow; being one of My disciples you should have friendliness and ingenuity enough to find some way of approach.'[2] We should be able to take our stand with Paul and say: 'As far as in me lieth, (as far as it depends on me) I am at peace with all men.'

CONSTRUCTIVE FORGIVENESS

The Lord's prayer has a straight, strong word to say on this matter which we should keep before us. It is no use praying for forgiveness unless we

2. Prof. J. A. Findlay, in *The Realism of Jesus.*

are prepared to practise it. A lingering bitterness towards others renders us incapable of being restored to fellowship with God.

Now listen to this: 'If ye forgive not men their trespasses, neither will your Father who is in heaven forgive you your trespasses.' What does that mean? Does it mean that God takes up an arbitrary attitude and declares that if we will not forgive those who have wronged us He will not forgive us? No! there is nothing arbitrary about God. In the day of my sin if I go to God and ask for forgiveness, and am willing to lead a revolution against myself, then God does forgive. But if, like some old Scrooge, I keep that forgiveness within my heart and fail to give it expression, then it perishes. This is sound psychologically. I must go out and share that forgiveness with those who have spoken ill of me, slandered me and spitefully used me, if I am to retain the sense of God's forgiveness. I must not shut the door against God and make it impossible for Him to bestow peace and tranquillity upon my spirit. Resentment and revenge are cheap and conventional, but forgiveness is constructive and God-like. We need not be afraid of forgiveness —it is a powerful grace which never finally fails, whereas retaliation is a poor, weak thing which never succeeds. We have all given cause for offence—dealt some wrong, inflicted some sorrow, and we have let the matter stand. We have been too proud to apologize, too cowardly to make amends. We have not made restitution. Others,

again, may have offended us and we have not forgiven them.   In either case life is impoverished.
If we have wronged anyone, therefore, let us make
restitution.   If anyone has wronged us, let us forgive him—for our own sakes as well as his.   And
when we forgive we do this tremendous thing—
we make God's forgiveness real to those who find
it difficult to believe.

Our Human Relationships

Jesus insists that our relations with one another
and with God are interlocked. He declares that we
cannot find God until we have made an honest
effort to come to terms with anyone with whom we
have for one reason or another lost contact. Before
we can get right with God, we must leave no stone
unturned to get right with men. We all know
people who profess to believe in God who would
be hurt if they were thought of as atheists and
would loudly deny it, but who in their human
relationships are as hard as flint, arrogant, unyield-
ing and implacable. They walk among us believing
in their god, but it is not the God and Father of
our Lord Jesus Christ that they worship.   One
has only to think of the character of Mr. Barrett,
in *The Barretts of Wimpole Street*, to confirm
this.

Shall we say, then, that if a man first loves God
he will then spontaneously love his neighbour?
The New Testament reverses the order. 'He that
loveth not his brother whom he hath seen, cannot
love God whom he hath not seen.' That is why
religion is unreal to many people. They can make

nothing of it, and they conclude that it must be a gift—possessed by others but not by themselves. They argue that just as a man who is colour blind sees the scarlet pimpernel as green, and just as a person with no ear for music cannot distinguish one tone from another, so people without the religious sense utterly fail to make anything of religion. They regard themselves as spiritually defective. But the clear teaching of Jesus is that everyone has a soul and religion is for every soul. There can be no realization of God if we are wrongly related on the human plane. A cherished resentment, a harboured grudge, an unforgiving spirit, an unconfessed wrong so put the soul out of focus that we cannot see God, but God became immediately real to many of us when we made restitution for wrongs done to others.

There is a very profound saying in the Book of Genesis: 'Ye shall not see my face except your brother be with you.' You remember that it was spoken by Joseph who refused to have any dealings with his brothers until they brought Benjamin along with them. His presence was demanded before they could get the bread they needed. And it is abidingly true that without our brother—the one whom we have treated badly, wrongly, inhumanely, sneeringly—we cannot see the face of God. Religion means right relations, a right relation towards God and man.

There is real teaching in that footnote of English history which relates how King George IV, desiring to receive the Sacrament, sent for the Bishop

of Winchester to administer it.   The messenger
having loitered by the way, a considerable time
elapsed before the Bishop arrived, and consequently
some irritation was manifested by the King. When
the Bishop appeared the King complained of his
delay in coming. Whereupon the Bishop explained
that he had come immediately when called.   The
King commanded the messenger to be brought
before him.   As he entered the room the King
rebuked him sharply and dismissed him from his
service.   Having done this, he said to the Bishop:
' Now, my lord, if you please, we will proceed.'
The Bishop, with great mildness, but at the same
time with quiet firmness, refused to administer the
Sacrament whilst any irritation or anger towards a
fellow-man remained in the King's mind. Whereupon the King, recollecting himself, said, 'My
lord, you are right.'   He then sent for the offend-
ing messenger, whose forgiveness and restoration
he pronounced in terms of great kindness. We are
not in the mood to worship God, nor is the soul
sensitive or receptive while we are offended or
have given offence.

The Way of Understanding

The insistence on restitution is one of the most
penetrating things in the Oxford Group.   The
Group holds that it is little use our getting the wisdom of what God's power and guidance can mean
in our lives, to surrender to God and attempt to
live a changed life, if that wisdom does not show us
that it is absolutely essential that we should get
understanding with those we love, work with or

come in contact with in our daily lives; and we cannot get that understanding with them unless we are honest about our wrong thoughts and actions in connection with them. Restitution is openly cutting the cord of sin which has bound us to the life of wrong we have lived in the past, and the only way of doing this is to acknowledge our faults to the people concerned and to pay back by apology or in kind if necessary that which we have taken from them.[1]

Restitution is righting to the best of our ability wrongs which we have committed in the past. Such restitution is itself a witness and brings men and women face to face with the Divine Spirit who makes such an unpleasant action possible. It is always hard to humble ourselves before others, and particularly so, if we do not know how we shall be received. It is harder still if we know that we shall be ill received. But it is the right thing to do, and if a man wishes to be a Christian it is his bounden duty to do so. The sincerity of our religion can be tested by our willingness to make restitution. If we have stolen we must restore, if we have lied and slandered we must do everything in our power to make amends. A Dutch farmer, who was changed through the Oxford Group Movement in South Africa, and who had employed native labour on his farm, called the natives together and spoke to them as brothers from whom he sought forgiveness and with whom he desired to share his new-found happiness in Christ.

1. *What is The Oxford Group?* By The Layman With a Notebook.

CHRIST ON THE ROAD

Professor Henry Drummond told a gathering
of University students in Edinburgh of a man he
knew who led a woman astray. 'He was fast and
evil then, but, a year or two after, he was changed,
and became what he is—one of the most prominent
men in the religious world. But through all his
success and apparent blessings there was the stain
and the shadow of that woman's life upon him.
Only three people ever knew about it, and it was
twenty years ago. He preached all through England and Scotland and Ireland, in the hope, I fer-
vently believe, that that woman might hear him
and be saved. Every prayer he prayed, he prayed
for her. Not long ago I was in London at a meeting which he was addressing, and after the meeting
a woman there walked up to him with bent head,
weeping. I saw them alone as they stood. That
was the woman he had searched for in the restitution of twenty years.' It is a hard path, but Christ
will go with us as we tread it. If we have missed
Christ on every other road we may find Him along
the road of restitution.

It is not the least part of the penalty of wrong
doing that sometimes it is impossible to undo it.
It is not always possible to retrace our steps and
undo the past, and there is nothing for it meanwhile but to leave it in humble contrition with God
who knows the road we have travelled and how we
were led astray, and who sees 'with larger other
eyes than ours, to make allowance for us all,' trusting that one day in a better world we may find the

opportunity which is denied us here. 'Oh, the anguish,' says George Eliot, 'of that thought that we can never atone to our dead for the stinted affection we gave them, for the light answers we returned to their plaints or their pleadings, for the little reverence we showed to that sacred human soul that lived so close to us, and was the divinest thing that God has given us to know!' What we can do is to give greater love to those who are about us. That is the restitution those within the veil would have us make. In the meantime there is the tremendous saving power of intercessory prayer.

In this matter of restitution the Groups recognize the importance of God's guidance. Mr. A. J. Russell admits that sometimes harm may be occasioned by unwise and unchecked restitutions. Answering the question: 'Why stir up trouble unless you are in a position to make amends?' he says, 'Each person must decide the thing to do on his own guidance checked perhaps by the guidance of others.' One of the guiding questions of restitution must be whether good will be accomplished by it or whether the one who has done wrong is simply seeking a personal release from the burden of his sin at the expense of the one he has wronged. Such restitution may add to the load which the victim is already bearing through the offence. But in nine out of ten cases in which wrong has been done to another some kind of restitution can be made and the acid test of our religion is whether we are ready to make it or not.

The Path of Power

George Muller, that shining saint who 'fathered' hundreds of orphan children in Bristol, was guilty of stealing in his youth, and he found that confession and restitution were the avenue to spiritual power.

Stephen Foot[3] tells of a party who went recently from Oslo to Copenhagen to apologize for their part in creating bitterness between Norway and Denmark. These men were members of the growing band in Norway who have accepted the challenge of the Oxford Group.

I do not wonder that Christianity does not make much headway in the world. How can peace come into the world while we who profess to want peace are poisoned with private hatreds and jealousies? These hearts of ours multiplied by millions explain why war with all its savage horrors keeps breaking out.

'If, therefore, thou art offering thy gift at the altar, and there rememberest thy brother hath aught against thee, leave there thy gift before the altar and go thy way, first be reconciled to thy brother, and then come and offer thy gift.' It means that if you are burning rubbish on your neighbour's washing day, and all her white sheets are smoked and begrimed, and you both lose your tempers and go at it tit-for-tat, your going to church will not soothe your ruffled feelings nor deliver you from your enemy. 'First be reconciled

3. See *Life Began Yesterday.*

to thy brother.' It is easier to give a coin to the collection than to give up the quarrel. It is easier to give a generous offering than to give up a grudge. Jesus warns us that a man who comes to Church like that is in danger. The peril is so desperate, the matter so urgent, he had better go out before the collection and be reconciled to his neighbour. What is he in danger of? Hell. Not a ready-made hell into which God hurls him, but the hell he is making for himself and where he is his own tormentor. 'Therefore' . . . 'Go' . . . 'Then Come.' It will be the same altar but not the same gift. The gift is never the same when he comes back—he gives not only something but someone—himself.

CHAPTER IV

DAILY CHECKING

THE FOUR ABSOLUTES

IT is a fatal mistake to live at random, presuming that all is well when in reality we may be deceiving ourselves. 'I am struck dumb,' writes Mark Rutherford, in his Journal, 'with my own ignorance of myself.' Every sensible man in business spends several days in the year checking his financial position and the result of his trading. If he does not make out an accurate balance sheet every year, he may be heading for financial ruin without knowing it; his expenses may be eating up his profits; people whom he trusts may be robbing him. If when a trader finds his way into the bankruptcy court, it is revealed that for years he has not taken stock, he is very severely censured and rightly so.

Whittier prays: 'Shine out O Light divine and show how far we stray.' That is the prayer of a man who is not satisfied to go on living a haphazard, unverified life.

When we speak of self-examination, it suggests tests. It implies the selection of standards of judgment by which we measure ourselves. The result of a man's self-scrutiny will depend upon the kind of test he applies. The Pharisee who thanked God that he was not as other men, compared himself with other men. The saints are not people who are better than the rest, but those who are trying to be better than they are.

The Group takes the four absolute standards of the life of Christ—Absolute Love, Absolute Purity, Absolute Honesty and Absolute Unselfishness. These are applied as daily tests of life in all its issues. This practice of regular self-examination in the light of Christ has proved to be of genuine practical value in our Christian development.

Is Perfection Possible?

Are absolute[1] love, purity, honesty and unselfishness possible? The answer is that they are the standard which Jesus Christ set for those who would follow Him: 'Be ye therefore perfect even as your Father who is in heaven is perfect.' No authority, however great, has any right to demand the impossible of us. But does Christ ever ask the impossible? Surely, it is a poor reflection upon His understanding of us if we think He would ever set a standard which would foredoom us to failure. In all His teaching He gave no precept which could not be carried into life. What, then, did He mean? If we read the saying carefully, the explanation is there: 'Be ye *therefore* perfect.' That word *therefore* evidently refers to what has been said previously.

'Ye have heard,' said Jesus, 'that it was said, Thou shalt love thy neighbour, and hate thine

---

1. There is no need to raise questions of metaphysics or philosophy and argue about the word 'absolute,' the real meaning of which nobody knows. 'Absolute' is used by the Group in the practical sense and means 'perfect.'

enemy. But I say unto you, Love your enemies
(i.e., let no one be excluded from your love), and
pray for them that persecute you; that ye may be
the sons of your Father which is in heaven: for He
maketh His sun to rise on the evil and the good,
and sendeth rain on the just and on the unjust.'

He warns His hearers against ordering their conduct by the prevailing standards—love your friends
and hate your enemies. If we love those only who
love us in return, there is no special merit in that.
Even disreputable people love their friends. If we
are friends only with the people of our own set,
that reveals nothing more than average good
nature, for the very heathen goes as far as that.
The world had been doing that for ages and yet it
was sinking deeper and deeper into misery and
despair. We are to be God's men. Our love must
be as catholic as His. Love must take the initiative
to produce a better relationship, for love is a creative thing. We must be full of love.

The mandate to be perfect like God, is often
regarded as an extravagant command. The finite
cannot reach the Infinite, man cannot attain the
absolute perfection of God. Truly, we cannot
emulate His wisdom or knowledge or power. But
that is not what Christ asks of us. Observe what
He *did* say. ' Ye therefore shall be perfect, *as your
heavenly Father* is perfect.' The personal note in
reference to the Father makes all the difference in
the world to our quest of perfection. The first
word to lay hold of in this saying is 'Father' and

then we shall understand the second word 'perfect.' We are to emulate our Heavenly Father whose life is in us, whose Spirit gives us life—we are to be possessed of His love which is kind to every member of the human family.

God is perfect as Father, that is what Christ says. And when is a father perfect? He is perfect when he loves. He is perfect when he loves His children with a perfect love. And love in our Heavenly Father is no more an abstract, distant thing than is love in an earthly father.

What Christ Believes About Us

When we say 'Our Father' we utter a very wonderful, comforting truth, but at the same time we accept a new responsibility, for His children must be like Him. The perfect life is simply a life of perfect love. Love is all and in all. Jesus said that the whole law is summed up in the one word *love*. It embraces everything, as St. Paul teaches in his glorious hymn to love (1 Corinthians 13).

And so we see that this neglected command, 'Be ye therefore perfect, even as your Father which is in heaven is perfect' is at once a challenge to and a revelation of us. That is what Christ thinks of us. That is what Christ believes us to be capable of. It is a tremendous affirmation of human values. It makes inhuman all the mean views of man's worth and destiny. 'Ye shall be perfect.' It was the boldest word He ever spoke, and 'He knew what was in man.'

Jesus does not compromise with our weakness but believes us capable of rising to great heights. 'Be ye perfect,' He says, 'Merciful, as your Father in heaven is merciful.' He has boundless faith in man's possibilities. His call is in itself a tribute. He calls us to take up the Cross and follow Him; to show the spirit of self-sacrifice, love, and heroism, and believes us capable of it. This call is not only a tribute, but bears witness to that link which, He felt, bound Him and all men together. 'Father' reminds us of an essential relationship that we have with Him.

We live so far below the level of our possibilities. There is a superlative in all of us if only we had the will to reach it. Nowhere do we get such a glimpse of our inherent greatness as in the presence of Christ. He reveals God to us and He reveals us to ourselves.

When Christ shows us what we may become, how can we go on being what we are? 'We needs must love the highest when we see it.' There is a tendency to be content with conventional goodness. Our worst enemy is not the devil but decency. We ought not to measure ourselves with this one or that one; but with God. Jesus sets before us the absolute standard of perfect love. The Church is sick to-day because we have diluted His demands and dulled the keen edge of His requirements. The Church is languishing through a failure to preach absolute Christian standards. Unless that ideal shines like a luring star, and unless we have hitched our wagon to it, all the services and church-going in the world will avail us little and we shall quickly grow weary of them.

The great exponent of perfection is John Wesley. He said: 'The work of God does not prosper where perfect love is not preached.'

The effectiveness of the Oxford Group is in no small measure due to the drastic process of confronting of men and women with an 'absolute' standard.

THE PARADOX OF PERFECTION

What Wesley understood by absolute love he well expressed in a letter to his brother Charles: 'By perfection I mean the humble, gentle, patient love of God and man, ruling all the tempers, words and actions; the whole heart and life.'[2] Of this state he says elsewhere, 'Further than this we cannot go: and we need not stop short of it.'

It must not be thought, however, that this high teaching overlooks the limitations of human nature. 'Christian perfection does not imply, as some men seem to have imagined, an exemption either from ignorance, or mistake, or infirmities, or temptations. . . . Neither in this respect is there any absolute perfection on earth. There is no perfection . . . which does not admit of a continual increase.'[3]

The only person who cannot be absolutely perfect is he who claims to be. Humility is essential to perfection. I have found people who claimed to

2. *Letters of John Wesley*, edited by George Eayrs, p. 83.
3. *Wesley's Sermons*, p. 562.

be entirely sanctified to be very difficult to live with. One man in particular who was for ever talking about sanctification lost his temper if anyone dared to disagree with him. Beware of self-righteousness which is only one degree worse than unrighteousness.

> 'They who fain would serve Thee best
> Are conscious most of wrong within.'

The paradox of perfection is that we can be perfect whilst we are still imperfect. When a child comes home with a hundred per cent. for his arithmetic exercise it does not mean that he is a perfect mathematician but that he has done that day's work perfectly. That is what our Lord means. He desires that we shall be perfect sons of the Father, having the hearts of sons, loving as only the children of God can love. 'Father, thou knowest that I love Thee.' This is the perfection of the son.

Dr. Stanley Jones illustrates the difference between perfect character and perfect love by the story of the father who came home after a long absence and was welcomed by his little boy with unbounded delight. As the father sat in the house, the little boy, scarcely able to contain himself with joy, came up to him, and eagerly said: 'Daddy, can't I do something for you?' The father, wishing to respond to the boy's eagerness, told him that he might bring him a glass of water. The little fellow, nearly tumbling over himself, ran across the room pell-mell to the water pitcher, poured some in the glass and some on the table, clutched the glass with a little finger on the inside of the glass, and then ran back across the floor with streams of water flowing from the glass and from the pitcher. When he pulled his finger out there trickled down the inside of the glass a muddy stream from his not very clean little finger. The father turned the glass around and drank every drop of it! The little fellow stood there rubbing his wet hands on his blouse and said: 'Daddy, can't I do something else for you?' Now that can hardly be called perfect service, but it can be called perfect love. Perfect character is a growth, but perfect love is a gift, and that gift can be obtained now—at the cost of our all. Perfection is not static but dynamic. Perfect love is a moment-by-moment holiness, a gay sanctity unaware of itself.

The Group insists on the indispensable necessity of a daily checking that we are absolutely yielded to love in thought, word and deed. The three other absolutes—Honesty, Purity and Unselfishness are qualities of Love. Like light, love is a compound. Just as the scientist takes a beam of light, and by passing it through a crystal prism, splits it up into its component colours, so love may be broken up into the elements of Honesty, Purity and Unselfishness.

Absolute Purity

Purity of mind and body are essential to perfect love. 'Blessed are the pure in heart,' said Jesus, 'for they shall see God.' There can be no outward purity unless we are clean at the heart's core. The carnally impure cannot see God, nor can they see others aright. 'And I say unto you, That whosoever looketh on a woman to lust after her hath committed adultery with her already in his heart.' To see a woman primarily as an instrument of sex is to have a wrong attitude to her human value. She is not primarily a woman, a potential wife—the first thing about her is that she is a living soul, and her sex is secondary to that. Jesus did not brand sex impulses as wrong in themselves; but He did assert that to regard any particular woman as if she were merely an object of desire was to degrade her personal worth, even though such an attitude goes no further than a thought.[4]

The New Testament paints sins in their primary colours and speaks straight out respecting adultery, uncleanness, fornication, lasciviousness and the like. But the impressive thing about the New Testament narrative is the widespread witness to men and women who had found victory over these sins.[5] In almost every Oxford Group there are people who have become strong because they have been made clean. Impurity is weakness—it unfits us for achieving God's Life Plan for us. I have often seen in shop windows an article labelled 'Slightly soiled. Greatly reduced in price.' Soiled lives are greatly reduced in value as constructive forces in the world. Purity is possible to every man and

4. See *The Realism of Jesus*, by Findlay.

5. An excellent book on personal sex problems is *Men, Women and God*, by Herbert Gray (Student Christian Movement).

woman no matter what their history or temperament. Purity is a gift—a quality of *given* love. Purity is positive and not negative. We do well to remember that there must be daily cleansing. We do not bathe once for a lifetime, but each morning, and so with every new day we must submit ourselves to spiritual cleansing and receive God's gift of purity.

ABSOLUTE HONESTY

We proceed to check our love in the quality of honesty. Love cannot live in a life of lying, thieving and shamming. That is why we must regularly scrutinize our motives, desires, fears and ambitions lest we come within the circle of moral disaster.

Deceit always begins in self-deceit, in what Plato calls the 'lie' in the soul. If we deceive others it is because we have first deceived ourselves. Every lie a man tells proceeds out of a lie he has first told himself. He deceives others much, but himself more. The lie recoils always and inevitably on the liar. He told the lie to save himself, to benefit himself, never doubting that he would profit by it, but in the end the lie did not profit him at all—on the contrary, it infected him, poisoned him, ruined him. To face candidly the truth of this position is to have our self-confidence shattered. No liar recognizes that he is a liar, for he evades the issue by the use of such terms as diplomacy, discretion or tact—mere camouflage. The thief does not regard himself as a thief, but rather as a dexterous artist in appropriation. The swindler defends his transactions as legitimate

business. Does anyone ever commit a sin acknow-
ledging it to himself as a sin? It is always due to
force of circumstances or a tidal wave of passion
or some grim necessity. The deadly nature of dis-
honesty is revealed by Christ's white-flamed
denunciation of hypocrisy in all its forms. 'I am
the Truth,' He said, and we constantly need to
test our lives by Him. Let us beware of blurring
moral distinctions. If we are true to Him, we shall
be honest and honourable in ourselves and we shall
not be false to any man.

Absolute Unselfishness

Further, if we are to be loving we must be absolutely unselfish. We can keep only that which we
give. Whosoever thinks to save his life by indulg-
ing it—refusing to plant a cross of sacrifice at the
red centre of his life—is not saving his life but
losing it. That is not a pretty paradox but an
inescapable law of life. It is a law of human nature
and works with absolute certainty. The self-
centred man does lose his life—the real life
dwindles and dies within him. Shakespeare makes
us see that in Shylock and Dickens in Scrooge. Both
characters were shrivelled-up men. We call the
selfish man mean and small. That is literally true
for he is cribbed, cabined and confined. Some
people who loudly demand the right to express
themselves have no self worth expressing. All
egoism is deliberate self-frustration, for the self
which shuts itself off from others shuts itself off
from the possibility of its own realization. If we

do not use ourselves we lose ourselves. Strength comes by spending it.

Every violation of the law of love sets up irritations, resentments, suspicions and jealousies which tend to break out in collisions of will.

Dean Inge reminds us of the Stoic saying that 'the selfish man is a cancer in the universe,' and remarks that the parallel is scientifically exact, since a cancer is caused by 'unchecked proliferation of cellular tissue by one organ independently of the rest of the body.' That selfishness is the bane of our fondest dreams and best plans and intents for the world to-day, few people who look on life with thoughtful eyes will be prepared to deny. Where self-interest is dominant it is impossible to have a true relation of personalities, whether it be in a small and intimate sphere like the home or in the larger extension where communities and nations are concerned.

Because self-indulgence is so subtle a sin we must hold our lives steadily in the light of the revealing Cross. We need to keep ourselves fit by regular self-denial. It is necessary for our own spiritual good that we should break the chain of our self-indulgence. It was not in a sermon, or in a lecture on morals, but in a *Textbook of Psychology*, that Professor William James said: 'Keep the faculty of effort alive in you by a little gratuitous exercise of it every day. That is, be systematically ascetic or heroic in little unnecessary points, do every day or two something for no other reason than that you would rather not do it, so that when the hour of dire need draws nigh, it may find you not unnerved and untrained to stand the test.'

Nine-tenths of our misery is due to self-centredness. To get ourselves off our hands is the essence of happiness. We do not find ourselves until we are thrown outside of ourselves into something greater than ourselves and set free.

It is sometimes asked whether the habit of daily checking may not lead to a morbid introspection. The question cannot be better answered than in Moody's words: 'If you want to be miserable, look within. If you want to be distracted, look around, but if you want to have peace, look up.'

How Can These Things Be?

Now we come to the crux of the matter. I have shown how Purity, Honesty and Unselfishness are standards of Love. The question remains: How am I to love? How am I to love perfectly? How am I to love as my Father who is in heaven loves?

The answer is: We learn to love, by receiving Christ into our hearts by faith. The love which we then have is not our love, it is the love of Christ expressing itself in us and through us. As St. Paul says, 'I live; yet not I, but Christ liveth in me,' so he might have said, and would have said had it occurred to him, 'I love; yet not I, but Christ loveth in me.' It is not merely that we are trying to approximate to a standard without and separate from us, but God begins to dwell in us. He assimilates us to Himself. We are not called to conform to an outward code, we work out a living principle that is within us. 'We are not saved by the love we exercise,' said Forsyth, 'but by the Love we trust.'

In a letter written in the year 1761 Wesley said: 'To say Christ will not reign alone in our hearts in this life, will not enable us to give Him all our hearts; this in my judgment is making Him a half-Saviour; He can be no more if He does not quite save us from all our sins. Who honours Him most? Those who believe He heals all our sicknesses, takes away all our ungodliness; or those who say, He heals only the greater part of it, till death does what He cannot do?' The logic of that is unanswerable.

Principal Rainy once turned upon his students at the communion table with this challenge: 'Do you believe your faith? Do you believe this I am telling you? Do you believe that a day is coming, really coming, when you will stand before the throne of God, and the angels will whisper together and say, "How like Christ he is"?' To believe less than that is to blaspheme Christ.

F

CHAPTER V

BE STILL AND KNOW

THE QUIET TIME

THE Oxford Group Movement is not a new religion; it is religion anew. Every upsurge of spiritual life in the history of Christianity has been the re-discovery and re-emphasis of neglected truths. One of the most valuable features of the Group technique is 'The Quiet Time.' Each member is urged to devote some time in the early morning to quietness, creating in the silence an atmosphere where one can be susceptible to Divine guidance and sensitive to the sway of the Spirit. The early morning is our own: after that the day belongs to other people. At the beginning of the day before we come into contact with others it is possible to have the mind illumined by unhurried reading of the Bible, by prayer and waiting upon God for guidance. Not only do we speak to God, but in the stillness we give God a chance to speak to us.

The Quiet Time is not a new discovery. It has been practised by thousands of people who knew nothing of the Group, but it has been featured afresh and brought to the notice of many who had not previously experienced the strength and joy of it.

The Groups are teaching multitudes of young people that prayer is, as Lancelot Andrews says, 'colloquy with God.' They are learning to be still and to wait for God. Many are finding a new joy in prayer and that it is something more than merely asking for things.

Learning Stillness

If ever a generation needed to learn stillness it is ours. We live as though our lives were intended to exemplify the theory of perpetual motion. We live in an intense, over-driven, nervous age, hurried and bustling, noisy and restless. Carlyle said of his day: 'The world is in a desperate hurry; woe unto the man who stops to tie his shoe-strings,' but what would he say of the greatly accelerated pace of to-day? Rush is taking a terrible toll of life. We are suffering from new diseases, not only of body but of spirit.

How seriously we need to learn stillness is expressed by that modern Lakelander, Hugh Walpole, in his story *Hans Frost*: 'I want quiet and silence. For a long time I've wanted those things, but I didn't know it. There are, I'm sure, millions of people to-day who want those things, but there is such a row going on that they can't hear themselves think. Someone soon will found a new contemplative order. It will have nothing to do with any kind of religion. It will simply be for people who want a quiet hour or two.' That very need is being met by the Oxford Group in the cultivation of the Quiet Time.

Like gamblers round a roulette table, we are too absorbed in this game of life. At break-neck speed we rush about altogether too busy to think of the consequences. Nevertheless, the consequences are emerging in a race of nervous wrecks in which idealism is submerged.

> 'The world is too much with us; late and
>   soon
>   Getting and spending, we lay waste our
>   powers;
> Little we see in Nature that is ours;
>   We have given our hearts away, a sordid
>   boon.'

That was what Wordsworth said amid the sequestered vales of the Lake District. What would he think of noisy, perspiring, rushing cities like Melbourne? Our mental life is equally hustled. There is no leisure for quiet, mind-building reflection.

Now, I know that we cannot slow down the pace of life. But, because life is such a rush, we must have oases of quietness, pools of silence. Action and reflection are necessary to each other. The more irons there are in the fire, the greater is the need to look after the fire. The greater the demands upon our strength, the greater the need to build up our strength. By quiet times we increase our efficiency, and fit ourselves for better work. We shall rise to the occasion when we learn how to sit still.

OVERSTRAIN A CAUSE OF RUIN

Stillness is a real cure for the brain-fag to which the inhabitants of a machine age are always liable. Overstrain is as fruitful a cause of moral ruin as alcohol. When we acquire the art of being still, we recover that peace and serenity which brings the whole being into harmony. We restore the rhythm in the billions of cells which compose the brain and body. The remedy for a neurotic age is so simple that we can apply it if we are willing to become as little children and learn.

A specialist in nervous diseases recently stated that in all his long experience he had not had a Quaker patient. You know the Quaker method of quietness before God. Two facts go together— constant retirement upon God in all things and an absence of nervous troubles.

In stillness there is both hearing and healing. That is a very beautiful story recording the walk to Emmaus, where two weary travellers are consoling one another in regard to the tragedy of the Crucifixion. As they walk, a stranger joins them and 'beginning from Moses and all the prophets, He interpreted to them in all the Scriptures the things concerning Himself.' The journey must have been a matter of hours and in the end their eyes were opened and they knew Him. Major John Findlay, in his book, *A Pilgrim in Palestine*, tells us that he made the journey to Emmaus by car in a few minutes! Ah, but he did not hear ' The thought that breathes, the word that burns.' Speed makes the world smaller; stillness makes it immeasurably larger.

We need hours of stillness to take our eyes off the glare of the road and enable us to see the beauty and the grandeur of the everlasting hills.

William James tells of the visit of a company of accomplished Hindus to Harvard, during which more than one of them confided to him the fact that the sight of faces, contracted, as they are, with American over-intensity of expression, made a painful impression. 'I do not see,' said one, 'how it is possible for you to live as you do without a single minute of your day given to tranquillity and meditation.' There are no Western religions, all the great religions have come out of the brooding East.

The Crowded Programme

We are very busy we say, the maximum amount of work has to be packed into the day's programme. Yes! but consider Jesus Christ. He had only three short years in which to accomplish His work as a teacher. But so much did He achieve, that John, after twenty-one descriptive chapters, despairs of recording it all and says: 'Now there is much else that Jesus did—so much that if it were all written down in detail, I do not suppose the world itself could hold the written records.' If any man could plead a crowded programme surely Jesus could, yet it was said of the garden on the far side of the Kedron that 'Jesus oftimes resorted thither with His disciples.' Again and again we read, 'He was alone,' 'He was apart.' It was because of the pressure of His work that He sought the soothing and sustaining stillness of the Father's presence. We shall never have more time than we have now and, if ever we are to know God, we must make regular appointments with Him in the secret place. I am not praising indolence nor extolling idleness; without industry we shall breed all the vices that stagnation brings. What I am pleading for is the renewal of our strength, the clearing of our vision, the deepening of our knowledge, that we may do bigger work and better work than we have done before. But there is a time for action and a time for quiet, and only in the proper balance of both can we preserve the rhythm of life. It is stillness for observation that we require.

'Be still and know that I am God.' There is a reciprocity between the two statements in that sentence. To know God we must be still. To be still we must know God. There must be silence in order to know God. The hurried mind and the distracted heart make a vital knowledge of God impossible. The ruffled lake gives no true reflection of the stars, but, when it is calm and smooth, it mirrors the firmament. When we are ruffled, troubled about many things, in a state of agitation and flutter, we are not conscious of God; there is no receptive quietness.

Why God Seems Unreal

'Be still and know.' We cannot know unless we are still. Philip Cabot, in sharing his own transforming experience,[1] says: 'The deepest form of worship is communion with God in order that our souls may be fed and the course of our lives directed in true accord with His will. For this the

1. The August *Atlantic Monthly*, 1923.

"seeing eye" and the "listening ear" must be developed by an utter concentration of all our spiritual powers—which requires time. Silent attention, with every spiritual sense alert, is the attitude of the worshipper who would hear the word of God.' That is very sound advice, based on the writer's own experience. It is no wonder that God and the spiritual universe seem unreal when we give them no opportunity to reveal themselves in us. Music would be unreal, and so would poetry and the arts to anyone who gave no more thought or concern to them than most of us do to the discovery of God in our lives. As Dean Inge has well said: 'It is quite natural and inevitable that if we spend sixteen hours daily of our waking life in thinking about the affairs of the world, and about five minutes in thinking about God and our souls, this world will seem about two hundred times more real to us than God or our souls. That must be so, however real and important the spiritual world may actually be. The fact that it seems unreal to us is no argument that it is unreal, if we only think about it occasionally. Things that we do not think about always seem unreal to us. Do not then argue that God is unreal because He seems unreal to you. Ask yourselves whether you have given Him, or rather yourselves, a fair chance.'[2]

The lack of spiritual energy in the Church is simply the symptom of exhaustion. A non-meditative religion is a shallow religion. This fact

2. *Religion and Life*, p. 8.

explains many things—the formalism and super-
ficiality of professing Christians, why so many
Christians are fighting a losing battle against their
temptations, why they lack power and influence
and fruitfulness, why the world is not being
changed. We hear and read the eternal truths of
God but we do not keep them in our hearts by
pondering.

We say, ' I believe in God the Father Almighty.'
Now, do we? Is there almighty power possessing
our lives? Have we not lost the sense of God in the
hurly-burly? ' Be still and know that I am God.'
The test of religion is the secret thing—the quiet
communion between man and God. One day we
may awaken to find that we have never known
God—though we have heard a great deal *about*
Him. Religious truths are conserved through
reflection. It is what we dwell upon that we live
upon.

It takes time to know God. It takes time to
believe. It takes time to know God's will. It
takes time to learn the mind of Christ. To know
God requires more than a hurried nod and a passing glance. Regular quiet times are essential.

God has a plan for every life. He will make
known to us His plan day by day if we give Him
a chance. But how can God teach us if we have no
time to sit in the school of stillness? God can
scarcely work an idea edgeways into our pre-
occupied minds. 'Oh! how rare it is,' remarks Fene-
lon, ' to find a soul still enough to hear God speak.'

IF WE HAVE LOST THE SPIRIT

Even when we pray we do not so much say 'Speak Lord, Thy servant heareth,' but 'Hear Lord, Thy servant speaketh!' Much of our praying is like speaking into the mouth-piece of a telephone without ever lifting the receiver to our ears. There is a voice always waiting to speak, but very few are able to hear it. You have not heard the whisper of it? That proves nothing, for thousands have heard it. But they may be deluded? Yes, but they may not. To those who heard, something distinctive was added to their personality—Moses, Samuel, Elijah, Amos, Isaiah, Gautama, Socrates, Paul, Augustine, Mahomet, Francis, Dante, Joan of Arc, Pascal, Bunyan, Wesley, Kagawa, Schweitzer. In the face of their testimony we ought at least to listen.

'If chosen men had never been alone
    In deep mid-silence open-doored to God,
No greatness had been dreamed or done.'[3]

A secondhand knowledge of God will not suffice. George Fox once said to Cromwell, 'What does it matter if we have the Scriptures, if we have lost the Silent Spirit that wrote them?' The Bible is not an encyclopædia about God, but a case-book telling how men and women like ourselves have found God.

It is in the Quiet Time that we come to know God personally and to be very sure of Him.

3. James Russell Lowell.

Yielded and supple before Him, waiting in stillness we hear, for 'Spirit to spirit doth speak.' The silence becomes a sacrament wherein God comes to us. We are never less alone than when we are alone.

Many of the astronomical discoveries of recent times have been made by means of photography. A prepared plate is laid in the base of the telescope, and the glass, turned towards the desired point in the heavens, is kept by clockwork in the right position, while the globe on which it rests is steadily revolving. By its own light the heavenly body records itself on this artificial retina, and things which the human eye cannot see are faithfully photographed and opened to leisurely inspection. In the same way the soul can subject itself to the quiet contemplation of the Divine Will and adjust its motion to those revolutions which, in times of feverish excitement, are forgotten or ignored. God, the soul, the purpose of existence, the proper objects of desire, the wisdom which moves and works in the universe towards the splendid goal, and the means by which our rapid and fitful lives can fulfil their purpose in harmony with the Divine idea are realities which never can be grasped in hasty glances or by feverish clutches. But by a process which God Himself maintains, they quietly reveal themselves to those who wait upon Him, and record their real though visionary outlines on those who have learned to meditate.

'Some there are that have no silence,' says Maeterlinck, . . . 'to them it is not given to cross the zone of revelation, the great zone of the firm and faithful light.'

LET GO AND LET GOD

'Be still '—' Leave off '—' Let be.' 'Desist from your own attempts and know that I am God.' God cannot do very much for us so long as we insist on playing the part of Providence to ourselves. Things begin to happen when we 'let go' and 'let God.' He is God—not you. We need what Wordsworth calls a 'wise passiveness'—we have to be still until our receptiveness is developed.

> 'I deem that there are powers
>   Which of themselves our minds impress;
> That we can feed this mind of ours
>   In a wise passiveness.
> Think you, 'mid all this mighty sum
>   Of things for ever speaking,
> That nothing of itself will come,
>   But we must still be seeking?'

The Quiet Time as taught by the Group is psychologically sound. It brings a new sense of order into untidy lives and a sense of tranquillity, but it is more than that. It is the way to the empowered life. We cannot create power, we must receive it.

Let me tell you how I spend my Quiet Time. First I read the Bible—preferably the life of Christ, the Book of Acts or the Psalms. I also make use of a hymn book which is a wonderful manual of devotion. I am greatly helped by a verse like this one of Bishop Ken's:

'Direct, control, suggest, this day,
　　All I design, or do or say,
That all my powers, with all their might,
　　In Thy sole glory may unite.'

I then kneel and wait in silence. Before I speak, I let God speak. I wait in self-forgetting silence, contemplating the presence of God. Then I recollect one or two attributes of God, but not more; that He is Love, that He is Spirit, that limitless spiritual forces are in Him and will flow out from Him to me and from Him through me to others; that He is truth and desires that I shall know His truth and see things as He sees them.

Good Listeners

Next I pray, using the Lord's Prayer as an outline.* I pray for spiritual development, growth in grace, strength for service and temporal needs. I expose my life to the four absolutes of the life of Christ—Absolute Love, Absolute Honesty, Absolute Purity and Absolute Unselfishness, checking up where I have failed—seeking pardon and power. Then I surrender the day to God that I may be completely at the disposal of His will. Surrender is not one life-long act but a daily renewal.

Finally, I wait again in passive silence. God speaks as well as listens. It is proverbial that the

* See my little book, *The Craft of Prayer*, p. 41 (The Book Depot, Sydney).

good talker must be a good listener. It is equally
true that the good petitioner must learn to listen.
How much of our praying is like the pranks of
little boys who ring door-bells and then run away
before anyone answers! While we wait in silence
God gives guidance. One of the best case-books of
daily guidance is the Journal of John Wesley. He
sought for it in his quiet time from 4 to 5 a.m. each
day. He prayed for it, waited for it and it was
given to him.

It is surprising how, while apparently thinking
our own thoughts, difficulties are cleared away,
problems solved, how doubt and uncertainty,
trouble and despondency and mental disquiet give
place to a sense of peace and joy.

Keeping a Guidance Book

The Group strongly recommends the keeping of
a Guidance Book wherein we write the inspired
thoughts that come in waiting. I used to smile at
this as a very kindergarten method. But I can
now testify that it is abundantly worth while. I had
no idea how well it works until I tried it. Suggestions are soon crowded out in the day's business
unless we make a note of them at once. There is
a page in Balzac's biography which tells how he
once mystified his tailor by ordering a pair of
trousers sewn at the ends to cover his feet. Finally,
the novelist explained to the poor man that he
wanted this weird garment so that he could slip
into it quickly in the middle of the night and be
kept warm while he wrote down the inspiration that

came to him. If inspirations are not captured and acted upon they soon evaporate. I wait there and set down as they come—duties to do, service to render, letters to write, witness to give, confessions and restitutions to make. The prayer that matters most is not petition but co-operation. In prayer we become fellow-workers with God.

It is absolutely necessary that this should be leisurely and unhurried. Haste is the death of prayer. I tell the simple truth when I say that it becomes so fascinating that one lingers in it and leaves it as reluctantly as one parts from a lover.

At first you may be bored. You will want to do something or talk to someone. You are probably an activity fiend, a noise drunkard. But keep on.

Of course, all sorts of irrelevant, material thoughts come tumbling into the mind. They do into everybody's mind. Do you remember Christopher Robin saying his prayers?

' God bless Mummy, I know that's right.
　　Wasn't it fun in the bath to-night?
The cold's so cold, the hot's so hot,
　　Oh! God bless Daddy I quite forgot.'

Distracting thoughts do come while the mind is being hushed. Don't worry about them. Just pause and then go on. The only real failure in prayer is to give up praying.

We all love bed. There is only one thing that will get us out in time—that is a greater love. The Quiet Time is so precious, the communion with God so real, the sense of tranquillity so sustaining that one is glad to be up and in it. Frankly, one does not always feel in the mood—there are times when I feel absolutely wooden—but the light comes and joy rises as I tarry. Miss it—and we become irritable and liable to storms of temper.

VARIETIES OF METHOD

If you are uncomfortable in kneeling, sit in a comfortable chair. The attitude is not essential— use whatever method best lifts you above time and sense. But remember that not one in a thousand can pray in bed and you are not likely to be that one. Many find it better to write their prayers rather than say them. Alfred Deakin, one of the greatest Prime Ministers Australia ever had, used this method. If you cannot be quiet at home start earlier for work and use a church or find a quiet walk.

I want to say to all who have known life's frustrations, its failings and its heaviness and weariness, who feel themselves unequal to life, surrender each day to God and begin with a quiet time. Jesus taught a fundamental lesson in mental hygiene when He bade us live one day at a time.

Hush thee! Hearken! 'Be still and know that I am God.' You will know God for yourself. You will find God. There are some sounds which become audible only when all others are still. In the old story of Elijah on the Mount, it was only after the wind and the earthquake and the fire had ceased that he heard 'the still small voice.' That story is a parable. It is only when the noisy shuttles of our workaday life are stilled to silence in the act of worship, that we are aware of that inward Presence which is 'the life of God in the soul of man.' Be still and know thy Maker for 'in the knowledge of Him is eternal life.'

'They that wait upon the Lord shall renew their strength; they shall mount up with wings as eagles; they shall run, and not be weary; they shall walk and not faint.'

G

CHAPTER VI

DON'T BE AN ASS!

GUIDANCE

'DIVINE guidance must become the normal experience of ordinary men and women,' says Dr. Buchman. 'Any man can pick up divine messages if he will put his receiving set in order. Definite, accurate, adequate information can come from the Mind of God to the mind of men. This is normal prayer.'

The crux of the Oxford Group Movement is its insistence upon the possibility and necessity of the guided life. It is easy to believe that God is interested in world tendencies, in the rise and fall of nations, but it is not so easy to imagine Him having a personal concern for each individual member of the many-millioned human race. A cross section of a thousand years of history reveals the hand of God in it, but the human unit is so insignificant in the scale of astronomical magnitudes.

Yet, from the beginning men have caught hints of an Eternal Power directing them—they have called it variously Fate, Chance, Destiny, God. Dim, hazy, uncertain, it may have been, but men have felt at times a sense of leadership. Socrates called it a 'divine somewhat.' He told his judges in his defence that 'the sign' was one which he had experienced ever since he was a child.

No one can read the Bible without being impressed by the constant references to Divine Guidance. Abraham was guided to leave Ur and become a pioneer pilgrim. We find that same sense of guidance in all the patriarchs—Isaac, Jacob, Joseph, Moses. A study of the life of David or of any of the other Old Testament heroes is a study in Divine guidance. So also with the prophets. There are numerous passages in the Psalms emphasizing the same experience. The inescapable conclusion is that the Old Testament teaches not merely a general providence, but a personal providence and that Divine guidance is available for individuals in all situations. We find the same evidence in the New Testament. The life of Christ was emphatically a guided life; at all times He is sure that He is fulfilling the Father's will; in every crisis He is guided. The Acts of the Apostles are really the Acts of the Holy Spirit. All this is very clear in the missionary work of Paul. His human purposes are often baulked by the contrary leading of the Spirit.

GUIDED SILENCE

There is nothing in the New Testament more dramatic than Paul's silent journey across Asia. He had planned the planting of Christianity in the stately commercial capitals of the Eastern world. But in each place he was 'forbidden of the Holy Spirit to preach the Word,' and trudged on in silence. 'The Spirit suffered him not.' As the Quakers say 'there was a stop in his mind against it.' And the result of Paul's obedience to that inward guidance was—Europe! It shifted the balance of power, and altered the face of the world. Benjamin Kidd has demonstrated that the great Western empires sprang out of that extraordinary silence.

There is scarcely a page of Scripture which does not witness to the fact of guidance. The plain promise of the Bible is that in all perplexities and anxieties we may expect illumination and direction.

Christian people generally accept the fact of Divine guidance but many believe that it only comes unconsciously. It is not possible, they feel, to know the will of God definitely in the present but only in retrospect. Newman sang:

> '*So long* Thy power hath blest me
> Sure it still will lead me on.'

The marks of God's providential leading as seen in retrospect are the grounds of our faith that in the unknown to-morrow He will see us through. That is gloriously true but it is not the whole truth. There is always a danger of limiting the possibilities of life to our own experience. There are more things in heaven and earth than our limited experience has discovered. Definite daily guidance *is* available to us.

One of our difficulties of believing that God cares for each of us is that there are so many of us— countless multitudes. But so to limit God is to make Him in our own image and to think of Him in terms of our limitations. It is difficult for us to keep individual interest in many people—therefore it must be hard for God!

> 'There was an old woman, who lived in a
>   shoe;
> She had so many children, she didn't know
>   what to do.'

Does that nursery rhyme represent our conception of God—that He has so many children that He cannot think of each one?

GOD AND THE INDIVIDUAL

We must grasp the principle that the greater the knowledge the more it breaks up masses into units. I was shown over a glorious garden recently—acres of flowers, shrubs, trees, ferns and mosses. All that remains with me is a joyous emotion of colour. But the woman who owns that garden knows every individual plant. A friend of mine collects butterflies. He has scores of drawers filled with these exquisite creations of varied sizes and colours. When I think of them I say to myself: 'Very beautiful' and perhaps recall a gorgeous one or two with vermilion and sapphire wings. But he knows the name of each one and the fine points of its structure and markings. When we think of God, we are confronted with a knowledge so vast that the attention to detail is amazing. He works not only in nations, but in individuals. Jesus assured us of God's personal interest in the individual. He told us that God not only counts heads but in His vivid way He said that He counts the very hairs on our heads. St. Augustine said, 'He loves every one

of us as if there were but one of us to love.'
I believe and indeed I know that the humblest of
us may have the personal, intimate guidance of
God in all the details of our lives. It is the privi-
lege of each one of us to be fully assured of the
will of God.

The Oxford Group stresses the reality of Divine
guidance in all the affairs of life—sacred and
secular, spiritual and temporal. God has a plan
for every life and He will reveal it to us day by
day when we fulfil the conditions.

The great task of life is to find out what that
plan is and how it is to be worked out. This is
where the Oxford Group Movement helps us.

God guides us when we are willing to do His
will. So the Group insists upon absolute surrender
to God—our selves, our sins, our will, time, possessions, ambitions, everything. He will guide us into
His will for us. Gladstone was constantly quoting
Dante's line: ' His will is our peace.' All our feeling of frustration comes from wanting to do something else with our lives than the purpose for
which God gave them to us.

An Old Testament Idyll

God can only guide us effectively when we are
going His way. In that lovely Old Testament
idyll Abraham sent his faithful steward on the
delicate errand of finding a wife for his son Isaac.
Upon that choice hung the welfare of his master's
home and we can imagine what doubts and fears
would assail him. He came at sunset to a village

well as the women were drawing water and was guided to Rebecca. This old retainer lived so near to God that he saw His hand in everything. The trifling action of a kindly woman giving him a drink and then watering his camels was to him a Divine leading. The presence of the maiden by the village well was providential. And it was then that he said a profound thing, 'I being in the way, the Lord led me.' He was treading the path of duty, doing the Divine will and the Lord led him in his difficult mission.

We all need guidance, for life is so strangely perplexing, appearances are so misleading, we are often at the cross-roads tortured by indecision. But we are not left to muddle through.

God's personal leadership, however, requires spiritual receptivity. The Quiet Time, reading the Bible slowly, praying and then lingering, waiting upon God, makes us receptive and sensitive to the Divine leading. Petition is not the whole of prayer. We must practise the other great form of prayer, the openness of the soul to God so that the light and power and grace which 'cometh down from above' may enter.

We have to become sensitive to God. 'The natural man receiveth not the things of God: for they are foolishness unto him: neither can he know them, because they are spiritually discerned.' God's guidance is conditioned by the material through which He works.

In the thirty-second Psalm there is this bit of 'horse-sense': 'Be not like mules and colts that do not understand the bridle, unbroken creatures that require a halter's curb or they will not come near you' (Moffatt).[1]   A colt has to be made to understand.   He kicks, bucks, rears, jumps the traces and has to be 'broken in' until he becomes susceptible to his master's will.   A mule is ever the symbol of stubbornness and stupidity.

When the Psalmist says 'Be not like mules and colts' he means very much what we mean when we say 'Don't be an ass.'

An old Egyptian proverb says: 'The ear of the boy is on his back and he hearkeneth when he is beaten.'   There are many people who are unaware of God in their lives until they are pulled up, checked by failure, adversity, disappointment, sickness and sorrow.   Don't be a mule destitute of moral sensibility.   God appeals to our reason. 'I have not called you servants, but friends.'

The Psalmist recorded this precious promise: 'I will instruct thee and teach thee in the way which thou shalt go.   I will guide thee with mine eye.'[2]   Between two people who are intimate friends a mere expression of the eyes conveys a message.   A glance is often enough to transmit a wish.   The flicker of an eyelid, a gleam that flits across the face conveys a world of meaning to one who is watching for it.   A child soon learns to read the heliography on his mother's face.   The language of the eye is the language of lovers.   Guidance with the eye, therefore, suggests fellowship,

1. Psalm 36: 9.
2. Psalm 36: 8.

a relationship between God and man, so sensitive and subtle and delicate that others would not appreciate it. God can guide us with His eye only if we are looking to Him.

The conviction of guidance in our outward life is in proportion to the realization of guidance in our inward life. 'Commit thy way unto the Lord; trust also in Him and He shall bring it to pass.' Having made that committal we become increasingly conscious of Divine guidance as the days go by. More and more do we become aware that our minds are fed from a higher intelligence.

HE SHALL DIRECT THY PATHS

'I will guide thee.' God honours that promise whenever we give Him a chance. It is a promise from God that He will give personal, private and unmistakable direction to those who open their lives to His control. When that chivalrous journalist, W. T. Stead, was offered the editorship of the *Pall Mall Gazette*, he went to talk it over with his friend, Dean Church. As they shook hands on parting, Stead said he was sure he would be Divinely guided. The Dean expressed some astonishment at his tone of certainty. 'I should feel swindled if I were not Divinely guided,' said Stead. 'How so?' asked the Dean. 'Why, I read in the Book of Proverbs, " In all thy ways acknowledge Him and He shall direct thy paths." I have acknowledged Him and I know I shall be directed.' The man who acknowledges God in his life can be certain of guidance.

How is guidance given? Not by an audible voice, not by the sudden flutter of white-winged angels, but through the working of our own minds. God acts upon the prepared mind. No one learned the secrets of Divine Guidance more intimately than George Muller, of Bristol. Here is his testimony: ' God guides us, not by a visible sign, but by swaying the judgment. To wait before Him, weighing candidly in the scales every consideration for or against a proposed course, and in readiness to see which way the preponderance lies, is a frame of mind and heart in which one is fitted to be guided; and God touches the scales and makes the balance to sway as He will.'

God has always honoured the human mind. Guidance comes to us in various ways; sometimes in answer to prayer, sometimes through the exercise of reason and judgment, and sometimes through the circumstances of life. It may be either immediate or mediate. When we suffer the Spirit of God to take possession of us He enlarges all our faculties of the mind. Reason, for instance, reaches its highest possibility when it is submitted to God. If we are to be guided by the Spirit we must live the life of the Spirit.

Sometimes God guides us by unreasoned impulses and at other times by unexpected inspirations and revelations. Experience is another way by which God guides us. Whenever Dr. John Clifford was perplexed he turned to the Gospels and read the example of Christ until some word or deed of the Master gave Him direction. Often we are led and we know not how—it seems the merest accident, a casual meeting, a sentence in a book. God uses all manner of means to give us the guidance we need provided we are prepared to follow His leading.

It is important to bear in mind that we are also directed by obstacles and delays. God closes every other door that He may open the right one. Livingstone wanted to go to China but God closed the door and guided him to Africa where he achieved his great missionary enterprises.

The Use of Guidance

Those who look to God for guidance accept God's plan, even though it cuts clean across their own purposes. We must beware of trying to *use* God instead of being used of Him. Guidance is not simply a convenient way of living, it is for life changing, and world changing. If guidance is sought and used for selfish purposes it will gradually become uncertain and unreliable. And the reason for this is in us.

The Group teaching on guidance has been severely criticized. Now we admit that some very foolish things have been claimed in the name of guidance. Any great truth or valuable experience can be caricatured. People have claimed that they have been guided to do and say things that we are sure God would not commend. Even those who listen most intently admit their liability to error. We are not infallible—not even the youngest of us! But we must not abandon such a precious practice because some distort it and we ourselves are sometimes mistaken.

The Group witnesses that guidance comes through a careful study of the Scriptures, a clear conscience, the cultivation of the mind of Christ in all things, the exercise of reason, illuminating thoughts, the circumstances of life and through the corporate fellowship of guided lives in the Church and the Group. Guidance must be checked by the highest standards we already possess; in the light of our duties and responsibilities to others and by the Fourfold Standards of the life of Christ.

I am told of a minister who surrendered. A week later he thought that he had guidance to go and tell a certain member of his congregation that he had long held very unfavourable opinions regarding his personal character. He went and shared his guidance, with the man, telling him, with evident relish, what he had thought of him. That interview threatened to end in personal violence—a striking instance of unchecked guidance. He was absolutely honest, but he was destitute of love.

Others have been known to make use of the word 'guidance' to justify a gay cancelling of solemn engagements at a moment's notice. Such a use of guidance may easily become a facile means of getting our own way, and justifying anything we want to do. The Group recognizes that guidance needs to be checked in various ways. If it is God's guidance it will be in accord with the mind of Christ revealed in the New Testament, and in harmony with the four standards—Absolute Love, Absolute Honesty, Absolute Purity and Absolute Unselfishness. And because the individual may be swayed by personal facts such as lack of knowledge, the Group further emphasizes the need for checking with other surrendered Christians. With these safeguards we may expect guidance as to what letters to write, visits to pay, restitutions to make and so forth.

We have to guard against thrusting our own will upon God when we pray to Him to guide us. We need also to be warned against too readily taking for granted any idea that jumps into our heads as Divine inspiration. A strong impulse is not necessarily a Divine guidance. It may arise from strong desire or a disordered imagination.

Checking Individualism

One of the commonest fears felt about simple faith in Divine guidance is that it will lead to unchecked individualism. That the danger is a real one it is impossible to deny. The Quakers, who know the power and peril of guidance, say: 'Inward guidance does not mean unchecked individualism, for the follower of the light will be continually correcting his first perception of it by a fuller experience, and by that of others who have followed it more faithfully.'[3]

A woman wrote to Gipsy Smith saying that she had thirteen children and had been guided that she ought to preach. He replied congratulating her on

3. *The Friend's Book of Discipline.*

her call to preach and pointed out that God had already provided her with a congregation! God will not guide us on a course which is absurd. If we are guided by the Spirit we shall be loving, judicious and rational, not flighty, precipitate and irrational.

How does guidance come? Why does not guidance come to you? It may be because you are an ass or a mule, lacking sensibility. If you are prayerless and careless God's message cannot reach you.

The story of Helen Keller may help you to understand. Helen Keller was only a baby when she became blind and deaf as the result of a serious illness. Loss of speech followed. There she lived in silence and darkness—hearing nothing, seeing nothing. Her mother lovingly and patiently tried to teach her to understand, but without success. A red-letter day dawned on her terrible night when Miss Sullivan, an apt and sympathetic teacher, came to her. Helen was not quite seven then. The morning after her arrival, Miss Sullivan gave her charge a doll to play with. Then after a while she spelt slowly into her hand the word 'd-o-l-l.' Helen was at once interested in the finger play and tried to imitate it and, when she finally succeeded in making the word, she was flushed with delight. So she began to learn the names of simple things. One day they went to the well-house covered with honeysuckle. Some one was drawing water and Miss Sullivan placed Helen's hand on the spout. As the cool stream gushed over her hand, she spelt the word ' w-a-t-e-r.' Helen knew then that water was the wonderful cool something flowing over her hand. Gradually her imprisoned spirit was set free. Miss Sullivan taught Helen about the beauty of the flowers and trees and sky and the sounds of bird music which she could not see nor hear. Everyone knows the subsequent story—how she went to the University, became a well-educated woman, a writer of books, and how she learned to speak.

But I think of Helen Keller's mother and father watching over her cot trying to signal to her, trying in one way after another to make her understand their love and not receiving so much as a smile of understanding or a word in response. Is not the little Helen Keller, blind, deaf and dumb an epitome of all mankind? God bending over us in infinite tenderness, seeking to direct us and we, deaf and blind, sobbing, 'Oh, that I knew where I might find Him!'

When a man keeps every avenue of his being open to Divine guidance, he acquires a firm conviction that he is being led, not always because of remarkable events but through daily, hourly, gifts of grace to meet every need.

How to Know the Will of God

'Be still.' That is the only way to know God. We are then tuned to receive God-given thoughts. We need a relaxed frame of mind, a freedom from tenseness and strain, fear and worry. Read the life of Professor Henry Drummond. The record of how this charming saint sought and found and followed the will of God is rich in suggestion for every man. Henry Drummond wrote on the fly-leaf of his Bible some notes on how to know the will of God: 'First, pray; second, think; third, talk to wise people, but don't regard their judgment as final. Fourth, beware of the objection of your own will, but don't be too much afraid of it. God never unnecessarily thwarts a man's nature and likings; it is a mistake to think that His will is always in the line of the disagreeable. Fifth, meanwhile do the next thing, for doing God's will in small things is the best preparation for doing it in great things. Sixth, when decision and action are necessary, go ahead. Seventh, you will probably not find out until afterwards, perhaps long afterwards, that you have been led at all.'

God guides—I give you my word for it, but you alone can prove it for yourself in the laboratory of your own experience.

CHAPTER VII

LIFE CHANGERS ALL

WITNESS

CHRIST'S strategy for the Christianizing of the world is one of the unexpected things in history. It seems, at face value, to be positively ridiculous. After three years of teaching, during which He had gathered round Him a group of twelve friends, He was brutally done to death on a Roman cross. His cause seemed wiped out and his enemies were crowing at their success in getting rid of Him and His gang. But what seemed to be the end of everything proved to be the beginning of everything. After His death He proved to His friends beyond all possible doubt that He was alive —powerfully present and vitally active.

In those three marvellous years He had revealed God, He had witnessed by word and deed to the love of God, He had given men and women victory over sin and opened to them the Kingdom of God. But He had only made a beginning. The news about God had to be given to the world. How?

Jesus entrusted this task to the group of eleven friends—one of the twelve had let Him down. They were an unlikely set of men—some of them uneducated, all of them slow to understand— 'slow in the uptake,' as the moderns would say. Read the story of the schooling of these men, at first so dull-minded and dense. At times the Divine Master almost lost patience with them. Not long before He died, they squabbled among themselves as to what they were going to get out of the Kingdom—who would be Prime Minister sitting on His right hand, who the Treasurer sitting on His left. He told them pointedly that whoever would be greatest in the Realm of God must be servant of all, and, to get it into their minds He gave an almost kindergarten demonstration, taking a towel and basin He washed their feet. There they were on the eve of His departure, an insignificant, uninfluential group, without status or backing. Their cause was discredited and as far as the world knew, their Leader had perished. Under such circumstances how could Christianity become a world force?

Christ's Plan of Campaign

'Ye shall be witnesses unto me both in Jerusalem, and in all Judea, and in Samaria, and unto the uttermost part of the earth.'[1] That was the plan of campaign. They were to begin where they were and then go out in radiating circles to tell the world what they knew of Christ and what He had done for them. Well, that is what they did. They began as a small 'team.' They declared what they knew of Him; how He had changed their lives and given them a fresh outlook and a new sense of values. They testified that He had filled them with

1. Acts 1: 8.

joy and peace, hilarity and courage. That is the clear and rousing story of the Acts of the Apostles.

Personal witness to Christ appeared to be a method too simple to overthrow the forces of materialism and agnosticism—and yet there stands the Captain's commission with the definite promise of power—a promise which was abundantly fulfilled on the Day of Pentecost with astonishing results. It was the simple witness of Spirit-filled men to the crucified, risen and ascended Christ that turned the world upside down, or should we not say—right-side up?

In his famous chapter on the cause of the wide and rapid spread of the Christian religion in the inhospitable soil of the Roman Empire, Gibbon, who was by no means a special pleader, assigns the first place to the fact that 'it became the most sacred duty of a new convert to diffuse among his friends and relations the inestimable blessing which he had received.'[2]

On all the great roads of the Empire these Christians were to be found, in strategic cities and in remote towns and villages. Tradesmen, artisans and travelling peddlers missed no opportunity of speaking a good word for Jesus. Though persecuted they could not be silenced; though driven from pillar to post they went everywhere telling, with enthusiasm, the good news of Christ.

'Into all these great divisions of the world,' says Dr. T. R. Glover, 'came men eager to tell the "good news"—generally quite commonplace

2. *Decline and Fall of the Roman Empire*, Ch. XV.

and unimportant people with a "treasure in
earthen vessels." Their message they put in
various ways, with the aphasia of ill-educated men,
who have something to tell that is far too big for
any words at their command. It was made out at
last that they meant a new relation to God by
virtue of Jesus Christ.... They were astonishingly
upright, pure and honest; they were serious; and
they had in themselves inexplicable reserves of
moral force and a happiness far beyond anything
that the world knew. They were men transfigured
as they owned. Some would confess to wasted and
evil lives, but something had happened, which they
connected with Jesus or a Holy Spirit, but everything in the long run turned upon Jesus.'

Justin the Martyr

Take one glowing example from the men of the
early Church. Justin Martyr—that hero soul who
placed his splendid gifts of learning at the disposal
of Christ and who was put to death for his faith.
He has told the story of his conversion in an
illuminating little book, known as the *Dialogue
with Trypho*. Like many other men of his age
Justin had sought for satisfaction in the philoso-
phies of the time. He had met with disappointment
after disappointment. He could not find the light.
He used to walk along a lonely road within sight
of the sea, pondering over the mysteries of life.
One day he was met by an old man, who told him
of the Jewish prophets and of the Christ in whom
their words had found fulfilment. 'Pray,' he said

to Justin, 'pray that over everything the gates of light may be opened to thee.' They parted and Justin never saw him again, but that word by the roadside brought him to Christ. Of his later life he was able to declare, 'I glory in being a Christian, and take every pains to prove myself worthy of my calling.' An old man spoke to a young man along a lonely road and the influence has lived for nearly 2,000 years.

The early Christian groups were hunted and harassed by cruel persecution. Meetings had to be held in secret. Yet they rejoiced and their persecutors complained that their teachings spread like wildfire. 'We are but of yesterday,' wrote Tertullian, 'yet we have filled your cities, islands, towns and boroughs; we are in the camp, the Senate, and the Forum. Our foes lament that every sex, age and condition, and persons of every rank are converts to the name of Christ.'

The twentieth-century world, deeply disappointed and disillusioned, bored and blasé—is wilting for this fearless witness to the living Christ who enables men and women to gain victory over their sins and empowers them to tell others what He has done for them and through them. Here is the secret of the remarkable power and world-wide growth of the Oxford Groups. In the Groups the cumulative effect of witness—not to themselves but to Christ—is demonstrated by lives transformed and by the energizing of nominal believers into vital, propagating Christians.

World Changing

How is the world to be changed? The world is an aggregate of units—every heart crammed with problems and yearnings. They must therefore be won as individuals. Andrew must find his brother. We must realize the pathetic need of men and women without Christ. In the last century earnest souls sought to save men and women lest they should go to hell. The urge to witness to-day is that men and women are already living in hell.

Christ committed the world task to His friends and they were to win the world through the power of witness. Christ works through human personalities. If you do not speak for Christ, who will? What if every Christian were just like you? A girl who went to China as a missionary, explaining why she volunteered, said: 'I seemed to see Christ standing alone among the heathen—dumb! No one to speak for Him, no one through whose life He could pour the love of His heart; waiting for someone to come to His side to be lips for him.' Truly, He has no hands but ours; no lips to speak, if ours are sealed. He is counting on us. There are those who cry, 'Christ is coming.' But lo! Christ is here, beseeching the surrender of your life and mine. Let us tell ourselves at each new dawn 'You are responsible for representing Jesus Christ to-day.'

The Christian Nobody Knows

I am not afraid of Christianity being blown up by its opponents but I am afraid of it being sat on by its friends. The trouble is with the 'Christian Nobody Knows.' A minister, who was coming to grips with a boy in his confirmation class, was met with the remark, 'Oh, I want to be a Christian like my father; nobody knows that he is one.' Nominal Christianity is useless. The dictionary meaning of nominal is 'unreal.' Peter denied Jesus with oaths and curses, but we let Him down by silence and concealment. We betray Him under social pressure. We shall have to give an account of every silence.

Sir Evelyn Wrench, founder of the Overseas League, says, in his autobiography,[3] concerning his long friendship with Lord Northcliffe: 'I always regret that I did not discuss the things of the spirit with the Chief. . . . In the hundreds of hours I must have spent in his company we never discussed the soul. I think he just left that side of life aside and his spiritual nature became atrophied. . . . He was much too busy "running the world" to bother about the world unseen.' If Northcliffe had been won for Christ the history of modern Europe might have read differently.

When I was a boy I used to be regaled with stories of Charles Peace, one of the most infamous criminals in the English calendar. My father used to tell me of seeing the black flag hoisted at the Leeds Gaol the morning Peace was hung. As he was led to the scaffold to expiate his crimes, the prison chaplain offered him what are called 'the consolations of religion.' The wretched man turned upon him and said: 'Do you believe it?

3. *Uphill* (Ivor Nicholson).

Do you believe it? If I believed that, I would crawl across England on broken glass on my hands and knees to tell men it was true! ' Peace was a clever man. If only he had been capitalized for Christ!

WITNESS BOX AND MARTYR'S FIRE

Only when we can transmit the Christian life can we be sure that we have it. ' Ye shall be My witnesses.' Witness comes from the Anglo-Saxon word *witan*, to know. A witness is summoned to tell what he knows. It is to a large extent a legal term. A witness is one who testifies to a cause; he is acquainted with the facts and upon his testimony depends the decision. Secondhand evidence is never so convincing. But this word has other meanings. It is a Greek word which really means ' martyr.' Our reservation of the word ' martyr ' to connote those who lay down their lives for what they know is significant. Real witness is costly. And the kind of witness which costs us little or nothing effects little or nothing.

' Ye shall be witnesses unto me both in Jerusalem, and in all Judea, and in Samaria, and unto the uttermost part of the earth.'

' In Jerusalem '—they were to begin at home; in Judea—among their neighbours; in Samaria—among those with whom nominally ' they had no dealings '; and even unto the uttermost parts of the earth.

This has been the strategy of Christian advance from the first days, and St. Paul, the great missionary pioneer, instinctively followed this principle in his attack upon the great world of Roman civilization. Paul's preaching was a tremendous asset but it was reinforced by a myriad men and women whose lives were changed.

When we witness—when we tell what has happened to us, we help others. Mark Rutherford tells of the revelation which came to him after he had published his *Autobiography*, of how an individual cry may voice a universal need. Thousands of letters reached him telling how he had stated just their particular case, while he imagined he had been stating only his own. When men and women 'share' what Christ has done for them, giving them victory over their private sins, they help others who are fighting the same battle.

There is a lady in my church who, when she came to me, was a hopeless, helpless, nervous wreck. She had lost the power to sleep, her mind was hot and fear driven. Life had ceased to be worth living. Then she came and shared all her burden—telling me of the way that she had trodden, the ache, the worry and the weariness of it all. I began to teach her slowly how to surrender everything to God—her life, her mind, her fears —and how to let Him undertake for her. Gradually the power of sleep returned and she now contributes to the philanthropic work of the Mission the money she formerly spent on sleeping-powders. But there came to me another woman, in a worse condition. I talked and prayed and sought to guide her into the way of healing peace.

I came to a point where I felt I could do nothing more. Then the inspiration came to me to let my first contact witness to her. She did so, telling of what she had come through, giving an assurance of victory. That is what witness does.

How Can We Be Silent?

There is a reticence in speaking about the soul. In some aspects it is a healthy instinct against hypocrisy. Christ Himself drew a contrast between those who conduct their religious exercises in public 'that they may be seen of men' and such as 'enter into their inner chamber, and having shut the door, pray to their Father who is in secret.' But we ought to recommend Christ in a simple, straightforward, natural way. Grenfell of Labrador relates how at a largely-attended afternoon tea, given by the Dean of an Oxford College, he spoke of Christ's attitude on some subject which came up for discussion. After the others had gone, the Dean took young Grenfell by the hand and said quietly, 'My dear Grenfell, we never speak of these things in general conversation.' Now, why should there be this conspiracy of silence about Christ? If we know the secret of victory, how can we keep silent? Have we really learned anything of vital Christianity worth passing on? A man is responsible to men for what he knows and responsible to God for telling them.

Henry Drummond, who had all the reticence of a Scot, once declared that he would rather break stones by the roadside than speak to a stranger about his soul. And yet Drummond was so oppressed by the sins and needs of men that he became an expert in personal evangelism. So great was his enthusiasm for Christ, so real his love for men, that he overcame his diffidence in speaking to men personally and he found that few men resent a tactful approach by one whom they believe to be seeking their highest good. A few days before Drummond died, Dr. Hugh Barbour played to him the old Scots melody, 'Martyrdom,' to which he beat time with his hand and joined in the words, feeble though he was:

'I'm not ashamed to own my Lord,
Or to defend His cause.'

When the hymn was sung, he said: 'There's nothing to beat that, Hugh.'

I know that some are halting at the threshold of surrender because they dread witness. The idea of introducing words about Christ in the ordinary ways of life seems so objectionable. Let me say that I understand that feeling and profoundly sympathize with it. But at every Group meeting I listen to the witness of young people who assured me when first we met that they could never do that sort of thing!

Then there is the fear of being crude in our approach to people. Our danger does not, as a rule, lie in the direction of outraging the laws of courtesy by inappropriate testimony, but in persuading ourselves that a later time will provide a better opportunity. We never speak to anyone without the side-tracking thought that we may be harming the cause by introducing it just then. We ought to give everyone with whom we are in contact the chance of a spiritual adventure. But witness is not by word of mouth only. There is no eloquence so persuasive as the life that is genuinely Christlike. What we want is men and women who will live their religion so that it is a natural, living part of themselves. Grace means beauty, it means, in fact, charm. To win some we must be winsome.

The Art of Catching Men

It is a great task to plan, to plot for the capture of a soul. Did not Francis Thompson think of Christ as 'The Hound of Heaven'? Set yourself like a hunter to win one man. Make him a target, a test case. You will need not only a hunter's persistence in pursuit but also the angler's skill, ingenuity and tact. 'I will make you fishers of men.' Clumsy handling loses many a fish. There is room for endless diversity of methods. Be willing and you will be used in terms of your own temperament. The witness will vary according to disposition. Conventional witness has little worth. There are hints in the first Corinthian Epistle that there had been an attempt on the part of some people to confine witnessing to certain standardized phraseology. St. Paul gave his strong ruling that the witness to Christ should be as varied as the idiosyncrasies of the men and women whom Christ has gripped. Charles Kingsley used to find out what men were interested in. He said, 'I try to catch men by their leading ideas, and so draw them off insensibly to my leading idea. And so I find— shall I tell you?—that God is really permitting me to do His work.'

One of the most successful personal evangelists I ever knew used to go round the slums getting men interested in gardening. Sometimes they had only half-a-dozen square feet of back yard and that a rubbish heap. Sometimes they hadn't even one square foot. In that case he would enthuse them with the possibilities of window boxes. He would give them seeds and plants, show them how to set to work, watching the main chance all the while, to drop in a seed for the Kingdom.

If we place ourselves at Christ's disposal He will use us. I can understand the atheist, I can understand the heathen, but I cannot understand the Christian in this day of the world's hopelessness, who is content to be a mere looker-on. Life changing on a colossal scale is the one hope of the world to-day.

Power is promised; power is available. Our Lord promises that just where we are defective He will supply the needed help. He told the apostolic group to tarry at Jerusalem until they received the power of the Holy Spirit. 'Ye shall receive power after that the Holy Spirit is come upon you.' The Holy Spirit is the Life giver and He alone enables us to become effective witnesses. 'When the Holy Spirit is come upon you,' says Christ. What does this mean except that we let Him control us—absolute surrender.

CHAPTER VIII

LO! HERE IS FELLOWSHIP

ONE man is no man. We need each other to realize ourselves. The story of human life on this planet is the record of man's slow learning of life's law of fellowship. First came the family, then the tribe, then the clan, and finally the nation.

The motives of fellowship are varied and they are not always marked by good will and pure intention. Sometimes fellowship is sought for mutual protection, sometimes for mere pleasure and often to gain power over others outside a particular class. But, whatever be the motive, fellowship of some sort is seen to be a sheer necessity of human life. Living to himself man is weak, poor, joyless, limited. In fellowship he becomes strong, rich, happy and expansive. It brings to him a greater fulness of life and a comradeship of spirit which means personal enrichment to all.

I remember hearing of a visitor to a large lunatic asylum who expressed astonishment at the small number of warders provided for the hundreds of inmates. When he mentioned the fact, the Superintendent explained why so few warders were needed. Lunatics never co-operate. Lunatics believe absolutely in themselves. William Morris was right when he made John Ball say, 'Fellowship is life; lack of fellowship is death; fellowship

is heaven; lack of fellowship is hell.' The supreme
need of the world is to replace the loneliness of
isolation and the rivalry of hate by Christian
fellowship on every plane of human life, individual, commercial, religious and international.

WE'RE A LONELY LOT

But fellowship cannot be manufactured or
organized. We cannot simply say: 'Go to, now,
let us have fellowship.' There cannot be brotherhood among unbrotherly people. No amount of
'getting together' will fuse us into fellowship.
An Oxford graduate tells how he used to be regularly disturbed by a gathering of men in the rooms
under his. The chief object of this little company
was the joy of getting drunk. They sang the kind
of songs so often sung by men who are tricking one
another with counterfeit companionship: 'For he's
a Jolly Good Fellow,' 'The More We Are Together,' 'For Auld Lang Syne.' The company
became increasingly rowdy. They usually broke up
about midnight. One of the men, who had kept
himself fairly sober, went up and sat by the student's fireside. They talked. 'You had a good time,'
said the first. He was answered with a laugh. 'Yes.'
Then, after a few moments' silence, he added:
'You know, friendship's impossible in that atmosphere. We don't really get to know one another.
We're a lonely lot.' And if some spiritually sensitive stethoscope could register the inward thoughts
of human hearts crowded together in superficial
merriment or dull sobriety, this is what we should

hear: 'We're a lonely lot!' What are many of our so-called pleasures save attempts to forget for a little while the haunted loneliness of the soul? Loneliness is the most terrible tragedy of the human spirit. It affects us with homesickness, nervousness and fear and makes us quarrelsome, sullen and irritable. There are so many who have no refuge; so many whom sorrow, disappointment or loss has left naked and destitute and whom loneliness besets like a black night unlit by a single star. 'Religion,' says Professor Whitehead, of Harvard, 'Religion is what a man does with his loneliness.' But the heart-breaking fact is that multitudes of people do not know what to do with their loneliness.

One of the greatest things the Oxford Group Movement is doing is to make fellowship possible. Everywhere, there are these happy people who have come into the comradeship of a world adventure. People who were living ingrowing lives have found a new power for making friends. To know one another on the other side of convention, with an intimacy which is only possible when we are surrendered to absolute honesty, purity, love and unselfishness, is a gladdening experience. There is no melting-pot like the fellowship of great things seen together, great things felt together and done together. The Groups are showing the way to a practising fellowship which departs from tradition and returns to the way of life and naturalness.

Fellowship is one of the great words of the New Testament as it is also one of the great facts of

Christian history. Now, the New Testament makes it quite clear that fellowship is in the Holy Spirit. When the apostolic benediction is being said at the close of a religious service and we hear the phrase 'the fellowship of the Holy Spirit,' I wonder what it conveys to us? Do we think it refers to having fellowship with the Holy Spirit? In a sense, no doubt, it does. But even more it means having fellowship with one another in and through the Holy Spirit. It refers to a certain quality, intensity and power of fellowship, which is indeed the highest form of human fellowship, and which is, as it were, created by the presence of the Holy Spirit in a group of people and by His action upon them. The New Testament fellowship was always warm because its flame was fed by Divine fires. To leave out the Holy Spirit is as foolish as to expect a train to travel swiftly when the electric power is switched off.

The First Team

Jesus never wrote a book, He organized no society, but He gathered a group of people united in closest fellowship to one another through allegiance to Him. To them was given the very energy of the Holy Spirit. They were a fellowship of mutual service through sacrifice and their task was to win all men to the fellowship of the love of God revealed by Jesus Christ. That was how Christianity started. It began with Jesus, who created a new kind of fellowship which included both sexes and all classes. It took in a Bolshevist (Simon the

J

Zealot) and his deadly opponent (Matthew the tax-collector). It found a place for the chief lady of the North Country—the wife of Herod's steward, and for a 'lost' woman—Mary Magdalene. The brilliant and glorious strength, the rich, full-blooded vitality of the first Christian fellowship lay in the fact that the team included such personalities as the gentle Andrew, impatient Peter, sceptical Thomas and visionary John. Jesus actually achieved the impossible, and created such a society as the world had never seen. In it all racial and political and national and social differences were harmonized, so that St. Paul could say: 'There is neither Jew nor Greek, neither male nor female, neither bond nor free, but ye are all one in Christ Jesus.' Do we realize what a miracle that was?

This close, intimate communion with Christ drew them to each other in mutual affection and mutual helpfulness; each seeking to share with the other his own resources in Christ Jesus. In those days to be cold to the brotherhood was a mark of disloyalty to the Lord. To be independent of the ·Christian society was not a mark of spiritual sufficiency; it was a sign of waning faith.

In the pages of the New Testament we can see this fellowship at work. The first picture of the Christian society after the day of Pentecost is that of a happy family, where all ate their bread with gladness and had everything in common.

How is it that so many sincere people, honest seekers, devoted churchpeople, have not found the radiance which they instinctively feel religion should produce? One reason is their lack of real spiritual fellowship—they have no congenial atmosphere in which it is easy to talk about Christ and share experiences with others.

'It is pitiable,' as Dr. James Denney once said, 'to see the substitutes that are found for fellowship in the Church and the importance which is given them, only because the real thing is not there.' You can be lonely in a congregation just as you can be lonely in a crowd. That many-gifted novelist, who assumed the name of John Oliver Hobbes, wrote in her diary in the heyday of her social popularity: 'The silence of my life overwhelms me. I dined out last night and met very charming people. I have seen visitors to-day . . . but the silence. I cannot face the loneliness of a crowded drawing-room, the host of mere acquaintances, the solitariness of the return. I must not be too depressing, but God only knows how I need a friend. . . . I choke my soul with work, and yet . . . and yet. . . .' Many a churchgoer could make a like confession. Little by little we have laid too much stress on the formal means of worship, to the neglect of that fellowship wherein the door of loneliness swings open and faith is fed in kindly company with those who had fears and hopes and sins like our own, but have found happy victory.

NEEDS THE PULPIT CANNOT MEET

There are heartfelt needs which the pulpit cannot meet. Sermons and books without fellowship are dead letters. What are the fears that haunt your heart, what the doubts that disturb your mind? What the failures that plague your conscience, what the visions that lure you on? Suppose you could talk heart to heart with sympathetic souls who have had those very experiences and found a remedy, what strength and hope would come into your life. Well, that is exactly the spiritual climate which the Groups provide.

A few years ago the Louvre authorities took steps to sell the magnificent pearl necklace bequeathed by Mme. Thiers, for had it remained on exhibition much longer, it might have perished entirely. Over thirty years ago the Thiers necklace began to suffer from a mysterious disease to which pearls are liable and which experts define as a form of starvation. Pearls thrive by contact with the human body and for this reason jewellers maintain that they must be worn if they are to retain their lustre. Otherwise they become shrivelled and unsightly. Why has our religion lost its lustre? Why has our spiritual power declined? Is it not because we have forgotten that faith needs fellowship and because we have tried to hold our faith apart from one another?

I read that on the day of Pentecost ' they were all with one accord in one place . . . and they were all filled with the Holy Spirit.' There is a power born in fellowship which seldom comes to the solitary soul. Read this surprising promise: ' I say unto you that if two of you shall agree on earth as touching anything that they shall ask, it shall be done for them of My Father who is in heaven.'

What does this mean but that when we pray together a vaster grace is available to us than our individual supplications can command? It clearly implies that concerted action in prayer produces a greater spiritual momentum than the sum-total of the units of power exerted by the same people praying separately. A company is greater than the aggregate of individuals who compose it. Then read this: 'Where two or three are gathered together in My name, there am I in the midst of them.' Hasn't our glib repetition of that promise blinded us to its mystery? When two or three come together in thought and prayer, the blessing realized is not simply an aggregate of their desire and petitions, but there is something more. They arrive together at a stage of power which they could not reach separately. Those who know claim that revelations are made, problems solved and moral power won which is far beyond the range of the separate soul.

Through the power of fellowship separate personalities blend in a society of friends that has a characteristic quality and a power of concerted action which increase the potentialities of the individuals. Such a book as MacDougall's *Group Mind* shows how great are the possibilities of increased, even of vastly and miraculously increased, power and activity in any group of people who are under the sway of a common purpose. Christ can work miracles of reconciliation through groups of men and women absolutely surrendered to His will for them.

The strength of fellowship comes from the fact that to men of limited view and partial capacity there is given immense enrichment of personal power and service. Sharing their lives and dedication to a common aim give added strength.

ONE-EYED RELIGION

The solitary unattached believer almost always becomes eccentric. We all need checking. We cannot see ourselves, but others see us plainly and can set us right. We see faults in other people while we are blind to our own. Even when we are living a guided life we need to be checked. Extravagances need to be corrected, self-will eliminated and the whole of our personality made sensitive to God.

Nothing could be further from the truth than to suspect that the Group encourages rank religious individualism. It is said that people claim guidance and then close their minds and become impervious to reason. This is not so, for there is regular checking among members. That, of course, is necessary. Almost everybody knows in these days why we have two eyes. A simple experiment provides the reason. Close the right eye and point to a given object. Hold the finger in that position, then open the right eye and close the left. You will find that the finger is pointing inches away from the object. And so vice versa. The two eyes do not look at everything from the same, but from different points of view. But the vision taken by two eyes helps us to see correctly and judge distances truly.

So different minds approaching a subject from their own angles produce a wider knowledge and wisdom than a single mind is capable of.

One Christian is no Christian. When John Wesley was acting as curate to his father at Epworth, he was told of a Lincolnshire villager who, even in those dark days, had won respect from his neighbours by reason of his goodness. Wesley, ready as always to learn even from the humblest, visited him. One sentence the old man spoke could not be forgotten: 'Sir, you wish to serve God and go to heaven. Remember, you cannot serve Him alone: you must therefore find companions or make them: the Bible knows nothing of solitary religion.' The words went deep, and, when the time came for Wesley to make provision for the spiritual needs of the awakened multitudes in the eighteenth century, he made fellowship the very foundation of the Methodist Society.

The riches of Christian character grow not by hoarding but by spending. Fellowship is not an end in itself but only a means to an end. It is very pleasant to meet and talk and pray in company with like-minded people but we have to watch lest it become a form of selfish indulgence. What we have found we must share—what we have seen we must tell. In a volume of early reminiscences, Mr. Frank Kendon has described the delicious sensations which the first cuckoo call of the year aroused. 'Before I was eight,' he says, 'I found I could not bear to hear it and remain alone. . . . It is terrible to be in an ecstasy of joy alone.' Many of us feel that same regret if we are alone in the presence of natural beauty, or as we listen to some soul-stirring music, or are moved by a great play or picture. We want so much to share it that it becomes a pain in the mind to be alone. What is this but the Spirit of God revealing to us that no enriching experience can be fully enjoyed until it is shared? Beauty, in every one of its manifold forms, thus lays on its worshippers a social liability to draw back the curtain for others to catch the vision.

The Purpose of Fellowship

John writes in his first Epistle 'That which we have seen and heard declare we unto you, that you also may have fellowship with us; yea, and our fellowship is with the Father and with His Son Jesus Christ.'[1]

'I thank my God,' says St. Paul, in writing to the Philippians, 'for your fellowship in furtherance of the Gospel.' That is what fellowship is for —the furtherance of the Gospel. The Oxford Group fellowship is committed to witnessing and life changing. Christ's message: 'The Son of Man came not to be ministered unto but to minister,' is the national anthem of the Kingdom of fellowship.

I say in all sincerity that as I see it the Group is God's gift to the world to meet the needs of the twentieth century. God has a plan for each one of us and He has a will for the world. That will can be known and realized if we will absolutely

1. Chapter 1: 3.

surrender to Him and be loving, honest, pure, and unselfish.   He will direct us, if we give Him a chance by making time to be quiet every morning. God will become real to us, we shall be cleansed and enter into God's sorrow for the world's sin and share His sympathy for the world's need. God's design will be made plain and all hindrances in us removed.   Christ's definite promise is that His Spirit will guide us into all the truth.

I feel it my simple duty as a Christian teacher to witness to what I have seen and felt of the new Movement which is spreading across the world because I want all to be in it, headlong for Christ.

As I understand it, Christianity is above all religious, and religion is not a method, it is a life, a higher and supernatural life, mystical in its root and practical in its fruits, a communion with God, a calm and deep enthusiasm, a love which radiates, a force which acts, a happiness which overflows. Religion, in short, is a state of the soul.

—Henri Frederic Amiel.

THE SECRET OF VICTORIOUS VITALITY

THE New Testament is the smallest book of
any religion in the world. What is the New
Testament about? The answer is one word—
Life. Not only that part of life which we think
of as religious, but life in all its relationships. The
problem of all problems, the mystery of all
mysteries is this thing which is so nigh unto us,
this thing which we all have but do not know what
to make of it—LIFE. 'Life,' says Bernard Shaw,
'is a thing of which it is important to have a
theory: yet most people take it for granted, and go
on living for no better reason than that they find
themselves alive.' 'Life,' says John Masefield, ' is
the daily thing man never heeds.'

What does the New Testament say about life?
It says that men and women are missing it, losing
it, wronging it. That is why they are unhappy;
they are not properly alive. And the condition to
which the New Testament addresses itself is this
—that what keeps people from life is sin. Whatever keeps us from God—who is Life—is sin.
Sin is not an arbitrary taboo set up to limit our
pleasures, but is whatever hinders us from the full
enjoyment of God, the Giver of Life. Separated
from Him we are like cut flowers, temporarily gay,
but doomed to wither.

It is told how President Calvin Coolidge, a man
frugal in speech, returned from a church service.

'What was the sermon about?' his wife enquired.

'Sin,' he said.

'What did the preacher say about it?' she asked.

'He was against it,' was the laconic reply.

All great souls have been against sin—they have protested against it and grieved over it. But the New Testament is the only book in the world that has a remedy for sin. The only remedy for sin, it declares, is the Son of God, who came into this world at a definite point of time in its history, in the likeness of men, who was tempted in all points like as we are, yet without sin; who taught and showed men and women how to live victoriously; who poured out the rich red wine of His life, His very blood, in a career of sacrifice which culminated in the Cross. It was impossible for death to hold Him and He triumphed in death as He did in life, shewed Himself unmistakably to His friends and continued to give them His victorious vitality.

The Life Giver

The New Testament is about Jesus; that is, it is about Him specifically; it is about Him above everything else. Those who write in the New Testament are concerned only about one thing— that those who read may see Him and be drawn to Him. 'These things are written'—we can hear them all saying it—'that ye may believe that Jesus is the Christ, the Son of God: and that believing ye may have *life* in His name.' 'I am come,' He said, 'that ye might have life and have it more abundantly.' 'Life' was His keyword; and of Himself He always spoke, not as One who preached life or explained it, but as one who gave it. Salvation, as He taught, is not primarily a protection against future punishment nor the guarantee of future reward. It concerns life here and now.

When we pass from the Gospels to the book which stands next, the Acts of the Apostles, it may seem at first as if the centre of interest has shifted, first to Peter and later to Paul. But it is not really so. Luke, the writer, certainly did not mean that it should be so. 'The former treatise I made,' he says, referring to the Gospel which bears his name, ' concerning all that Jesus began both to do and to teach '—*began* to do and to teach. Then what is the inference? Surely, that this new writing is the story of that which Jesus continued to do and to teach; so that if Luke himself, instead of someone else, had had the naming of his book, he might have called it ' the Acts of Jesus through the Apostles.'

This Ecstasy of Liberation

The writers of Gospels, Letters and various other treatises which compose the New Testament are all concerned with this life, this new power to live, this ecstasy of liberation which had come to all sorts and conditions of men and women. Apostles went forth on heroic journeys, suffering hardship and persecution to witness to it. Groups composed of freemen and slaves, aristocrats and artisans, who had found in Christ victorious life, sprang up in cities and towns.

St. Paul waded through a world reeking with moral filth, but he never lost heart because he was in fellowship with Christ who caused him to triumph and who could change the world. In a world upon which disgust and loathing had fallen there came this newness of life. The pagans were impressed by the freshness, the vitality, the joyousness of the Christians. Their men were pure and honest, their women had the bloom of virtue upon them, so that one pagan was led to exclaim: ' What women these Christians have! '

Now all this is ancient history and we have been too much inclined to leave it at that. But groups of people across the world have discovered to their amazement that this thing *works*—that it is verifiable to-day. They have proved that Christ is continuously active and gives this new quality of life to all who will surrender their lives to Him day by day and make a quiet time each day in which they become receptive to the infilling of His Spirit.

' Be of good cheer,' said Jesus. ' I have overcome the world. And lo! I am with you always.' He knew that by another set of sun He would be hanging upon the Cross between two thieves. Was that victory? Most surely it was. He made the very cross an asset and made use of it for His own purpose. He made it His throne so that it has become the cherished symbol, the very sceptre of sovereignty. Such was the quality of this life in Him.

He Who Gave and Still Gives

'Be of good cheer, I have overcome the world.' What does that matter to us? For Him to tell us who fail that He did not fail might seem to mock us. But He felt that what He had done had a significance for His followers beyond that of being an inspiring example.

'I have overcome the world and I will come and put my overcoming Spirit into your weakness and fill you with my own victorious life and be in you the overcoming and conquering power.' Christ's victory is ours, and we are victors in it, because He is more than an example, because He is the Son of God, who gave Himself for us and gives Himself to us, and dwells in us, our strength and righteousness. We have to take the step of faith which sets us in the circle of Christ's victory. Recognize that He has overcome sin; therefore this very sin—this personal sin of ours has been overcome. What happens? The soul is charged with a strength not its own.

Ruskin said that 'the Christian pulpit fails in its effect, because it speaks so much of what men must do to obtain salvation and so little of what God has done to give it.' The Christian has to receive the victory of Christ. It is no longer a lonely fight, doubtful to the end. Just as after the abolition of slavery every negro was born into a world made free, so the victory of Christ means that we are in an emancipated world. But some slaves could not believe that they were free and were afraid to leave the old plantations. And there are many of us living on as whipped slaves when we might be free.

VICTORY OUT OF TRAGEDY

There is no promise that life will be 'roses, roses, all the way.' 'In the world ye shall have tribulation,' said Jesus. No blinking of difficulties there. Hardy has painted the stark tragedy of life in his novels, but there he left it, he showed no way out; the rest is silence. Jesus alone brought tribulation, peace and cheerfulness together and showed us how to win victory out of tragedy. He discovered it in His own experience and He communicates it to those who share His spirit. 'In the world ye shall have tribulation.' Jesus did not guarantee immunity from pain and sickness, loss and death, monotonous toil, blighted hopes and disappointed ambitions but He did promise such victorious living, such hilarious joy as nothing could defeat.

'The religion of Jesus means these three things: Victory over sin, victory over self, victory over suffering. It is in the fitness of things that Jesus cried out, " In the world ye shall have tribulation, but be of good cheer, I have overcome the world." This is cheer indeed, a cheer that has faced all the facts of life—good, bad and indifferent—and has let those facts say their worst, and then in the face of it all bursts into laughter—a gay, glorious victorious laughter—a hallelujah chorus out of unhallowed conditions.'[1]

The Book of Acts reveals how this life was available. St. Paul may or may not have seen and heard Jesus in the days of His flesh, but he proved the victorious life of Christ in his own experience. The seventh and eighth chapters of his letter to the group in Rome are to a large extent autobiographical.

GLORIOUS LIBERTY

The seventh chapter portrays, with remarkable subtlety of analysis, the strivings and struggles of one who is convicted of sin, and who seeks to attain to a good and serviceable life. But we see only the helpless movements of some struggling creature that would rise. Beaten and baffled, writhing in the mire, the soul at length sinks into utter despair of self. 'Wretched man that I am! who shall deliver me out of the body of this death?' But then a new note is struck: 'I thank God through Jesus Christ our Lord!' Help has come into his helplessness. The secret of a new life thrills his being. Now he can rise; now he can soar and sing. 'All things are possible to him that believeth.' The eighth chapter unfolds these new possibilities. It is a pæan of praise. We hear the buoyant and rhythmic tread of victors. Just because 'there is now no condemnation,' because he is already 'in Christ Jesus,' he breathes a new atmosphere, and is vitalized with a Divine energy. 'What the law

1. *Christ and Human Suffering*, Stanley Jones, p. 142.

K

could not do'—what no commandments, no resolutions, no strugglings could accomplish—is now fulfilled by the impulse and inspiration of the Spirit. Instead of the laboured servitude, there is the willing surrender that finds its congenial element in 'the glorious liberty of the children of God.' Against this obedience great forces are at work; but on behalf of this obedience greater powers are working, and are working so mightily that even the things which threatened to be evil, and only evil, are compelled to work for good. So mighty are these powers, and so effectual is the deliverance already wrought, that we may well be 'persuaded that neither death, nor life, nor angels, nor principalities, nor things present, nor things to come, nor powers (of whatsoever sort), nor height, nor depth, nor any other creation (of unexpected circumstance or condition), shall be able to separate us from the love of God, which is in Christ Jesus our Lord.'

MASTERING THE WORLD

In a letter which St. John wrote to the Christian groups in the cities and towns of the Empire, he said, 'And this is the victory that overcometh the world even our faith' (1 Jn. 5: 5). What did he mean by 'the world'? We read in the glorious Genesis poem of creation that 'God saw everything that He had made, and, behold, it was very good.' Jesus loved the world and His teaching is full of exquisite reference to fields and flowers, birds and trees, sunsets and seasons. Jesus was no ascetic.

He was very different from Luther, who in his monkish days kept his eyes closed as he sailed down the Rhine lest the beauty of the landscape should seduce his heart from God. To Jesus the world was sacramental with God's presence. ' The earth is the Lord's and the fulness thereof.'

But as a matter of experience we know that even the good things which God has made, if used unspiritually may separate us from Him. As Emerson said, ' *Things* are in the saddle and rule mankind '—whereas they should be the stirrup to help us to mount nearer to God. By ' the world ' John means ' the arrangement,' the sum total of the forces of nature, our human bodies, our social relations, the conditions of our existence, all things which are either in themselves averse from life or may become so by our undue absorption in them. We may enjoy all things good and beautiful in the world and sincerely thank God for them, but even these things may lead us from God if they become our master-passion and side-track our surrender to Him. But other elements of the world are in themselves hostile to God—' the lust of the flesh, the lust of the eyes, and the vain-glory of life ' (1 Jn. 2: 15-17).

Thus, on the one hand, we may turn the good things of the world into spiritual foes by making their pursuit our chief object: on the other hand, we may succumb to the deadening influence of things that tend of themselves to our injury—its pomps, its noise and show and glitter. But victory over the world is possible. We may so triumph over it that the pure, good things in it shall only increase our grateful love to God, and not enthral our hearts. Its empty vanities, its toys, its seductive offers will have no attraction for us.

This faith in the living power of Christ is the victory—the strength which enables us to master the world, ' using the world but not abusing it.'

The Sorrows of Life

And now read this: ' Who shall separate us from the love of Christ? shall tribulation, or distress, or persecution, or famine, or nakedness, or peril, or sword? As it is written: For thy sake we are killed all the day long; we are accounted as sheep for the slaughter. Nay, in all these things we are more than conquerors, through him that loved us.'[2]

The enemies conquered are ' tribulation, anguish, persecution, famine, nakedness, peril, sword '— gathered into one word, the sorrows of life. If these worked their full effect upon us they would break our faith in God. But the life that is surrendered to God is victorious over them. So far from alienating us from God they bring us nearer to Him: so far from destroying faith, they strengthen it: so far from withering our soul's harvest, they multiply its ' peaceable fruits of righteousness.'

We not only prevent these things destroying us, but we actually convert them into allies. The ' more than conquerors ' seems to mean the conversion of an enemy conquered into a friend and helper. Just as the American Indians thought that every scalp

2. Romans 8: 35-37.

taken increased the warrior's strength, and that the power of the slain foe entered into the brave's arm, so these tribulations may in very truth empower the spirit. 'In all of these things we are more than conquerors through Him that loved us.' It is something to be a conqueror. No one knew that better than the Romans in whose memory there still remained a vivid impression of the triumphs of Pompey and Cæsar. But to a little group of 'Christians' the apostle had the insight to ascribe the title 'more than conquerors.'

Yet victory is not *our* achievement, for these things would naturally sour us and make us cynical. We conquer through 'Him that loved us.' Horace Walpole said, 'Life is a comedy to those who think, and a tragedy to those who feel,' but, as Forsyth added, 'it is a victory to those who believe.' On that last night of His earthly life Jesus took the cup, the symbol of His poured-out life, and said 'Drink ye all of it.'

'Drink,' He said, 'for the whole world is as red as this wine with the crimson of the love of God. Drink, for the trumpets are blowing to battle and this is the stirrup cup. Drink, for I know whence you came and why—I know when you go and where.'[3] Truly He is the Way, the Truth, and the Life.

Christ can turn our defeats into triumphs. It is told of Morphy, the world-famous chess player, that he once saw a picture of a youth playing chess

3. G. K. Chesterton, in *Omar and The Sacred Vine.*

with Satan, doomed, to all appearance, to inevitable defeat. Morphy procured board and chess men and set the pieces out as they were in the picture and then with one move changed what looked like certain failure into positive triumph. And Jesus can take the problem of our lives, show us the next move and make us victorious.

Then there is victory over death. 'Thanks be unto God who giveth us the victory through our Lord Jesus Christ.' It is a shout of triumph. 'I am the resurrection and the life,' says Christ. 'He who believes in Me will live even if he dies.' In His resurrection Jesus became a death-defying, death-defeating, life-giving Spirit. The seeming victory of the cold earth is no victory at all. The victory is with life. I have written enough to show that the New Testament is the book of victorious life.

Throw off Defeatism

Hugh Redwood ends his book, *God in the Slums*, with these words: 'The Christian religion must throw off its defeatism. Christ is not struggling for victory. The victory was won 1,900 years ago. That is what the ordinary man needs to be assured of, the daily victories of the living God.' It is this mood of victory that we need. Our religion has been too much the religion of effort. Instead of saying 'I can do it' we must affirm that 'God can do it.' 'He is able to do exceeding abundantly above all we ask or think.'

I have watched a fly struggling in a spider's web
—frantically flapping its wings, striving to dis-
entangle its feet, twisting and pulling, but all in
vain, for the spider has come and wrapped it round
and round until it was helpless. But many a time
I have rescued a fly just in time as the spider came
hurrying out of his den. And Christ can set us
free from the toils that entangle us, for

'He breaks the power of cancelled sin
   He sets the prisoner free.'

You may have resigned yourself to a poor, low
level of living; and have come to acquiesce in
things as they are. You may have practically no
desire for a victory which you have found to be
impossible. Just such a case Christ came to meet.
He gained the victory of His Cross exactly to
secure the victory which, you have told yourself,
is impossible. Your only fault is despair, or, what
is the same thing, unbelief. You are not allowing
Him to do what He came to do and has indeed
done. You lie in your helplessness and hopelessness while He is always holding over you the
crown of victory and the palm which is the symbol
of rejoicing. 'I know,' you say, 'but I cannot see
it, I cannot grasp it. The thing seems too simple or
too remote or too intangible.' My reply is: 'The
simplicity of it is intentional, the remoteness of it
is due to your not facing it and realizing it. It is
only intangible because you do not grasp it.'

I say it again and yet again, the victory is yours
if you will take it; it is achieved if you will believe
it. Faith, in this connection, is simply receptiveness.

The pledge of victory is conditioned by your absolute surrender to Christ. Practise the Quiet Time every morning. ' Be still and know that *I am God* '—not you. Come into the fellowship of those who have overcome sins and problems similar to your own and who can witness to victory. The Divine very often comes to us through the human. That was why Christ was born in Bethlehem and took upon Him the form of a man that He might speak to us in human words and heal us with the touch of a human hand.

MY TEXT

*If a man will do His will, he shall
know of the doctrine, whether it be of
God, or whether I speak of myself.*[1]

A PREACHER during his lifetime takes many
texts but this text took me. The day
when it leapt up with living power from
the black and white of the Bible page and appre-
hended me—that is a red letter day in the calendar
of my soul. This great saying saved me, like a
lamp put into my hand in a night of darkening
doubt and blank bewilderment. It showed me the
way—the way through the maze of conflicting
creeds and schools. It gave me the key to my problems. This word of Christ saved me and it has
kept me. I have lived with it—I have shared it
with scores who have come to me with shattered
faith seeking light and guidance. I am confident
that it will bring certainty to any man or woman
who applies it to life.

The setting of the saying is this: Jesus had gone
up to Jerusalem and begun to teach in the Temple.
He made a profound impression. The virility of
His teaching, His sure knowledge of God and man,
His insight into life, were like the tang of a fresh
wind suddenly blowing into the laden humidity of
a limp day. Even the Pharisees were unable to

1. St. John 7: 17.

deny the power of His teaching. Smitten with amazement they said, ' Where did this man get His knowledge of God—He was not educated in our schools.' They were at a loss to account for His wisdom, His method, His obvious understanding of things Divine and eternal. ' How knoweth this man letters having never learned? ' they enquired. They knew His history. He was the carpenter's Son. He was certainly not a graduate of any of the Rabbinical schools, and yet He showed an acquaintance with the Scriptures which left the ablest of the Rabbis breathless.

The Test of Teaching

It was natural that any one making special claims should be regarded with special caution. Jesus knew quite well that He would not be readily received on His own valuation. He knew how bewildered they were. His astonishing wisdom was not learned in any of the schools, nor was it self-originated; it came from God. ' My teaching,' He said, ' is not mine, but His that sent Me.' But what evidence could He give for such a staggering claim? There had been many false prophets who claimed to be the spokesmen of God. Anyone who makes such a claim must expect to be challenged. Jesus did not object to such a challenge. It was one they had a perfect right to make. He met it. He told them how they could verify His statements and test the truth of His teaching. ' If any man willeth to do His will, he shall know of the teaching, whether it be of God.'

There Jesus gave them and us a transcript of His own history, the secret of His inward experience. 'You ask where I obtained my knowledge of God? I will tell you. I obtained it from doing God's will and that way is open to all earnest minds.' What Jesus said to His hearers was plainly this: 'Put this truth that I teach into practice and you will know for yourselves whether it is of God.'

'How can I prove that Christianity is true?' Only by subjecting it to the test of life. Things which are insoluble in thought often become clear in practice. Truth is proved in action, not by reason alone. That was the witness of Jesus and it is what multitudes need to learn to-day. Men and women of keen and eager minds have thought themselves to a standstill. Science has opened a new universe; criticism has subjected the Bible to ruthless enquiries. Men do not know what to believe or where to take hold. Christianity does not depend upon any one or all of the Churches, not upon any system of theology, not even on the Bible. Christ drives straight to the heart and demands the test of experience.

ACTION ILLUMINES THE MIND

We often make the mistake of thinking that we cannot act until we know. We forget that often we cannot know until we act. We cannot sit down and logically prove Christianity to ourselves first and then begin to practise it. The practice and proof of it go hand in hand. Action illumines the

mind. 'Do the truth you know,' said George Mac-
Donald, 'and you shall learn the truth you need to
know.'

If any soul is bewildered by many things in the
universe and in life, and even in the Christian
scheme of belief, the best thing that soul can do is
to begin to do the will of God, the highest known
good, to obey the demand of conscience and take
Christ at least as the Master of the art of living.
Then gradually he will feel in himself the reality
and divinity of the eternal things revealed through
Christ. So the essential experiences of Christianity
are repeated in us and the essential doctrines shine
with morning freshness.

'If any man will do His will he shall know
of the doctrine whether it be of God.' All that
really matters in the Bible for us, all that is worth
contending for, is what can be reproduced and veri-
fied in our own experience. What are the doctrines
of God? According to Jesus they are the doctrines
that can be lived.

Dr. L. P. Jacks has well said that 'no moral
truth is ever learnt, or the meaning of it even
faintly understood, until we are actually engaged
in putting it into practice.'

Action must precede understanding, knowledge
is the consequence, not the cause of doing. Jesus
did not say: 'Here is a scheme of thought and
doctrine. I have explained it in detail and
answered every possible objection. Now I charge
you to make your life accord with the doctrine
which your intellect has approved.' Not thus did

He teach us; but rather: ' I have set before you a way of life. I have revealed it to you by word and by example. Now test its worth by experiment. At whatever seeming cost of sacrifice, live this life. Do that which I have shown you as God's will. For thus only shall you arrive at knowledge, thus grow sure that the words which I have spoken unto you are true. " If any man willeth to do His will, he shall know of the teaching whether it be of God." '

Shall we delay until as a result of prolonged intellectual investigation we satisfy ourselves at every point of the validity of Christ's claim? Well, hear Carlyle: 'Doubt of any sort cannot be removed except by action. On which ground, too, let him who gropes painfully in darkness or uncertain light and prays vehemently that the dawn may ripen into day, lay this other precept well to heart, which to me was of invaluable service: Do the duty which lies nearest thee, which thou knowest to be a duty! Thy second duty will already have become clearer.'

'If any man willeth to do His will he shall know of the doctrine.' Let him, with all his doubts, and with all his fears, plunge himself into the midst of life's realities, and he will discover in the doing of the will of God whether there is a God or not. But if he stands outside the doing, he will never know the doctrine. Only as he crosses the threshold of the doing, will he know the realities, the ultimate meanings of life. This, it seems to me, is backed up by the whole attitude of Jesus Himself.

Have you ever thought how little Jesus argues? Jesus never undertook to reach the heart of man through the intellect. Jesus never tried to convince anybody against his will. He always tried to bring the will into the field, to release it in the direction of the thing He knew to be good. He always tried to keep the intellectual difficulties of His audience and His disciples in the background and to centre attention upon the doing. If only He could get men to do right, they would think right.

A French infidel once said to Pascal, 'If I had your principles, I should be a better man.' 'Begin with being a better man, you will soon have my principles,' was the philosopher's apt reply.

The Organ of Knowledge

I propose now to take this text for a walk up the street and hear what it has done for other lives. Frederick W. Robertson, that gallant knight of God, that royal preacher, took this text when he preached before the Assizes at Lewes in 1852. He called that sermon, which is one of the really great sermons in print—'Obedience, the Organ of Spiritual Knowledge.' The title indicates the substance of the discourse as a few sentences will indicate: 'What is Truth? " Study," said the Jews. " Act," said Christ, " and you shall know." A very precious principle to hold by. . . . " He taught not as the scribes." . . . They dogmatized, " because it was written," stickled for maxims and lost principles. His authority was the authority of Truth.

... He commanded men to believe, not because He said it, but He said it because it was true. .... Obedience and self-surrender is the sole organ by which we gain a knowledge of that which cannot be seen.'

Behind that sermon is the preacher and Robertson preached it out of his own heart. He had passed through a period of heart-sickening uncertainty; he had trodden the via dolorosa of doubt with bleeding feet. 'But in all that struggle,' he said, 'I am thankful to say the bewilderment never told upon my conduct.' Mark that. 'In the thickest darkness, I tried to keep my eye on nobleness and goodness, even when I suspected they were will-o'-the-wisps.' He kept his will steadily doing the will of God from day to day and he came to know the doctrine as we all may do if we persevere and grow not weary in well-doing.

In the year 1845, we find that courageous Christian, Charles Kingsley, tossed on a sea of doubt and clinging to this great saying of Jesus like a shipwrecked sailor holding on to a raft for very life. He writes in a letter: ' " He that doeth the will shall know of the doctrine whether it be of God." Were it not for that text, I think I should sometimes sit down " astonished," and pray to die and get it all cleared up.'

Then there is Horace Bushnell, one of the strongest intellects, one of the most lovable saints that America has given to the world. Bushnell lived near to God. When, towards the end of his life the Rev. Joseph Twichell, who was Mark

Twain's minister, visited him, they sat out together under the starry sky. Bushnell said, 'One of us ought to pray.' 'You pray,' said Twichell, and Bushnell began his prayer with the words, 'I have remembered all the way that Thou my God hast led me.' Then, said Twichell, 'burying his face in the earth, he poured out his heart, until I was afraid to stretch out my hand in the darkness lest I should touch God.'

Another minister said to this radiant saint, 'When Christ sees you nearing the gate, Dr. Bushnell, I am sure He will say "There comes a man I know."' The great theologian's eyes flashed as he replied, 'And I think I can say that I know Him, too.'

The Clue to God

How did Bushnell become so sure of God? For answer we must go back to the days when he was a tutor at Yale. He was the most popular teacher in the University but all at sea religiously. There was a spiritual quickening in the College but he was unmoved and a number of students were sheltering behind him. The minister who was leading the revival sought him out and challenged him: 'Professor Bushnell, if these things that I am preaching are true, wouldn't you like to know it? If Christ does change men who trust Him, and forgive them and put a power superhuman into their lives, wouldn't you like to know it?' And Bushnell, after a thoughtful pause, replied, 'Certainly I would like to know it, if the thing be reliable.' Then said the minister, ' You can know it if you will just be candid.' ' How? ' ' Take Christ's own challenge and here is that challenge: " If any man will do His will he shall know of the doctrine whether it be of God." . . . Take that clue and you will find God.'

Pacing his room one day, there came up suddenly the question, ' Is there no truth that I do believe? ' ' Yes,' he answered himself, ' there is one, now I think of it; there is a distinction of right and wrong that I have never doubted. Have I then ever taken the principle of right for my law? No, I have not; consciously I have not. Here then,' said he, ' I will begin. If there is a God, as I sometimes hope there is, and very dimly believe, He is a right God. If I have lost Him in wrong, perhaps I shall find Him in right.' And the young Yale professor dropped on his knees, chose to do the right he knew, and with what results I have shown.

Then there is that remarkable English scholar, Professor George John Romanes. He had been brought up under narrow evangelical influences but, when he went to the university and was confronted with the new doctrine of evolution, he was unable to reconcile the findings of science with the doctrines of the Church. He forsook his faith with bitterness and tears and out of the pit of unbelief he sent forth a cry calculated to arouse those whom he thought to be the dupes of Christianity. That cry was his book, *A Candid Examination of Religion.* Years passed, and there fell by chance

L

into his hands a little book of science, describing
the researches of a missionary in China, Gulick by
name, revealing an intimate knowledge of nature
and a deep appreciation of the bearings of the
current evolutionary hypothesis. Romanes was
surprised, and wrote to Gulick asking him how a
missionary, who believed in the supernatural,
could make such a valuable contribution in the field
of pure science.

Gulick replied that he applied to the field of
science exactly the same method he was accustomed
to use in the domain of faith, proving all things
through personal experience. This was a new
thought to Romanes. He had never conceived that
the claims of religion could be found false or true
by definite experiment. He realized that he
had started at the wrong end. He began to
seek God by doing His will. He found that will
most clearly expressed in the life and teaching of
Christ and he began seriously the slow and patient
effort of living the life and letting the belief take
care of itself for the time. Starting with no confession of faith, but with a very definite confession of
duty he worked his way into the clear sunlight of
faith in Christ. He withdrew his former book and
wrote another, *Thoughts on Religion,* in which he
took as his keynote the words of John Hunter,
' Do not think; try.' ' Christian belief,' he said,
' is more due to doing than to thinking.'

' If any man will do His will he shall know of
the doctrine whether it be of God.' This is the

scientific method. The text book formula is veri-
fied by laboratory experiment. In the spiritual
world we must fulfil the test conditions and make
the experiment which leads to the experience of
God. If the scientist describes to me an experiment
which has to be carried out in a darkened room
and I try it out of doors, am I entitled to deny the
scientist's conclusions because the experiment didn't
work? If God is not real to us, if we have not
experienced His Fatherhood and proved His
providence, let us candidly ask ourselves whether
we have honestly fulfilled the test conditions?

THE TREE OF DECISION

Lady Henry Somerset, the gracious lady who
worked so hard in the cause of temperance reform,
passed through her dark time like the rest of us.
The heavens were brass. God seemed dead. He
was, at any rate, deaf to her beseeching. She had
no heart to go on with the tasks which she had
undertaken in His name. But while she stood
under a great tree on her estate at Reigate, the
tree of decision as she subsequently called it, the
tree which is still shown to visitors, she heard a
voice which said, ' Live as though I were, and you
will know that I am.' Live as though God were,
and we shall know for certain that He is, as Lady
Henry Somerset did. Live the life. Think the
kind thought. Speak the kind word. Do the kind
deed. Give the witness. And in due season, if we
fail not neither grow weary in well-doing, we shall
' know in whom we have believed.'

One of the voices of our time has been Dr. R. F.
Horton, who turned his back on a promising career
at Oxford to found a Christian group at Hampstead
which grew into a fruitful church.   In his *Autobiography* he tells the story of a remarkable influence in his life.   When he was sixteen he went to
spend a three-weeks' holiday with a friend at Halifax.   That visit had a determining effect upon his
religious faith, on the choice of a career and on his
character.   Arriving in Halifax he went with his
friend's family to a temperance demonstration and
there met the eldest sister. He tells what happened:
' As we sat on the sunny slope and watched the
procession pass—I looked up and saw that face
which from that day forward shone upon my life
with a light which seemed to come from another
world.   It was a very beautiful face . . . but the
countenance was all aglow with pity for the suffer-
ers whose lives were brought before her by the
procession.   All this I saw at once, the powerful
influence of woman as the guiding star and inspiration of a man's life had flowed in upon me and
rapidly flooded my whole soul.'   She was at that
time twenty-two.   The next day, walking home
from church she turned brightly to him and said,
' I think we shall be friends? '   Recognizing at once
what it meant to him, she told him that she was
engaged to be married and that they could only
be friends if he recognized the nature of her
friendship.   To have her friendship and interest
was all that he desired.

For forty years, until she died, that woman was the guiding star of his life.

Soon after she was married, she went with her husband to visit Dr. Horton, who was then in his first term at Oxford.

An Oxford Testimony

'I was telling her of all the difficulties,' he said, 'and she quoted a verse which up to that time I had never noticed: "If any man willeth to do His will he shall know of the doctrine whether it be of God...." She spoke out of the experiences she had gained in her own inward wrestles for faith. Those words sank into my heart. I got the conviction which has deepened ever since that Christ's doctrine is not established by external arguments.... I had not thought it out then, but the principle was discovered which leads to the conclusion that Christ's doctrine is not proved by an infallible Bible or an infallible Church. But when a man wills with all his might to do God's will, he finds that the doctrine of Christ is of God.'

If we wait until every problem is solved or the date of every portion of the Bible fixed, that will not make us Christians. We become Christians when we set out to do God's will. Let religion be lived and it will cease to be doubted. The only way to know truth is by transmuting it into life. Truth is proved not by logic but by life. 'The truth is what will work,' said James, of Harvard.

Doing is the condition of knowing. 'Whosoever loveth is born of God and knoweth God, for God is love.' God is not reason but love, and it is therefore as impossible for reason to know God as to see a picture with your ear. 'The world by wisdom knew not God.'

There is not a philosopher from Plato to White-head but may be clean bowled by the questions of a little child. The humblest man who actively trusts Jesus Christ knows more of His providence, sees more of His glory than the most learned theologian who is faithless. 'If any man. . . .' I have known many simple saints who, without any schooling, were very sure of God and with remarkable mental clarity. They clung to the right; they prayed, they learned obedience. The paths which some philoso-phers have missed have been found by charwomen. Mary of Bethany and the fishermen of Galilee knew more of God than all the scholars of Jerusalem.

You will never think rightly if you live wrongly. If you will to do His will—desire sincerely to do it—if only you will here and now make a beginning, the light of God's truth will shine in your mind, the assurance of God will come to your inmost soul. You will know God for certain.

APPENDIX C

MY WITNESS

It has not come within the scope of this exposition to chronicle the exploits of the Oxford Group Movement. The witness of changed lives and the international spreading of the Group may be read in the rapidly growing library of books on the Movement. But I cannot refrain from telling the story of my own heart and witnessing to what the Group has done for me.

I surrendered my heart to God in Sunday School days and I have never doubted the validity of that covenant, however unworthily my part of it has been lived. Two formative experiences which followed were firstly, the Whitsuntide when I came to know the Holy Spirit as a personal power realizable in the willing life and not merely the third person in an obscure doctrine of the Trinity, and, secondly, the day when I saw the Kingdom of God as the Divine Order yearning for expression in this world. It was the Kingdom of which Jesus was forever speaking, likening to the homeliest things such as baking and mending that the simplest might understand. When I saw the Kingdom I had a fresh vision of Christ and a new understanding of His mind. The time of my ordination to the ministry was the occasion of deep heart searching and unreserved consecration to the will of God. I had no other motive than to serve Christ and make

Him real to men and women. The professional parson I kept as a warning of what not to be.

God used my ministry to a degree that kept me humble with gratitude. At an unusually early age I came to the Cathedral Church of my denomination in the State and now for ten years, I have faced every week one of the largest regular congregations in Australia. Here is a Church that speaks to the nation. Here is a Church expressing its faith in Christly deeds, supporting a hospital for unmarried mothers, a home for girls, a training farm for a hundred orphan and problem boys, a hospice for homeless men, a sunset home for elderly ladies; maintaining mission sisters who work in slum areas, feeding and clothing thousands of people every year. This surely was a congregation and a programme of practical Christian service to rejoice the heart of any minister. And yet, as I look back to the days before the Group came, I can see how an insidious world sickness had affected me. I had preached a new world after the war—the old order with its inflamed nationalisms and absurd militarism was dead and gone. Then the reluctance of the nations to disarm, the ineffectiveness of the League of Nations for want of spiritual support, and finally the economic blizzard known as the depression, with its cruel unemployment, made me sick at heart. How could the world ever realize the Kingdom of God? I could scarcely bear to think about it. When I did, I took refuge in Luther's saying: 'I tell God that if He wants the world saving He must do it Himself.' It was an illicit shelter. I found myself wishing that my lot had been cast in other days—that I might have lived in the seventeenth century as rector of some quiet English village with a handful of people to love and teach with leisure for studious ways. Yet all the time I went on with my work, filling the flying minutes, preaching at the highest level I could attain and preaching in terms of my personal experience of Christ. Not for a moment did I relax my zeal to win souls for Christ and there were regular conversions in the fellowship of prayer which we held regularly after evening service. In my early ministry, I had realized that a Church with a declining spiritual birthrate is a dying Church, no matter how healthy its present membership may be. People came to see me frequently for spiritual counsel and I was used to lead hundreds of them to Christ. All the while I loved to pray and out of my experience in prayer came the little guide book, *The Craft of Prayer*. The needs of the world were heavy upon my heart. I was frequently upon my knees with an open atlas interceding for all nations and peoples. Human wisdom had failed. The problems of the world were too great for the statesmen of the world. There were plans in plenty but so little power.

And then one day there came to this Melbourne, twelve thousand miles from Lakeland, a strange evangelist. God keeps up His surprise power and here was something totally unexpected. The Gilbert and Sullivan Opera season was announced

with Mr. Ivan Menzies cast for the leading roles.
He came and booked his room in one of the hotels.
Quietly he began to change people in the hotel.
A hard-shelled journalist who went to interview
him was changed. Ivan Menzies had been caught
by the Group and surrendered absolutely to Christ.
He is not a broken-down actor who has turned to
religion as a last resort. He is a young man at the
height of his powers as an exponent of Gilbert and
Sullivan's operas. People wrote letters previously
by the basketful to thank him for cheering them up
and saying that his own happiness had infected
them. 'But,' he confesses, 'I was not always as
happy as I looked, nor as pleased with what I saw
of myself inside as those who took me at face value.
Why? Well, there were several reasons. One was
that I really had problems in my life. Another was
that I was a little uncertain of my ultimate goal,
and so my direction and purpose was undefined.
Again, although outwardly I was ranked a successful man, yet inwardly there was a good deal of
failure.'

Then Ivan Menzies met a Group friend who
told him of the miracle that had happened to him.
He had found truth at last for himself, and an
answer to his own problems, and, therefore, to
those of the whole world.

'He so intrigued me,' said Ivan Menzies, 'that
I felt I could not relapse into whole-hearted
paganism again until I, too, had tried to see
whether this would work for me. Because, I
reasoned, if it would work for me it would work

for anybody. So I sat with him far into the night being absolutely honest about myself. I carefully weighed the consequences such a step might entail —loss of vocation, sneers, sarcasm and even ridicule.

'Well, I didn't break my neck, I didn't make a fool of myself. But I did make the most wonderful discovery of my life, that Christ could do to-day for me what He said He could do if I would let Him WITHOUT COMPROMISE. My problems vanished one by one. My happiness became real and permanent . . . not just the frothy effervescence that comes from hitting a few high spots. A new power, purpose and direction came into my life, and oh, wonder at last, I could really bring others to happiness if they were willing—not give them a palliative, but a real answer to their heart's desire. For myself, the big question mark vanished absolutely. At last I was able to live above irritation, provocation, impatience, jealousy, and all those thousand and one things that had been tripping me up. In other words I found love—the love that passeth all understanding. I found what men all over the world say they are looking for— the Way to God.

'Can you wonder then at my ardour to communicate to my fellow-men what God has given me?'

Well, this changed man set about life changing in Melbourne. He went out to Pentridge Gaol and witnessed there, and among those whom he led to Christ was a prisoner serving a life sentence for murder. He won men and women in the University, his fellow-actors, doctors, solicitors, society women, Communists and the most unlikely people. What he accomplished reminds me of Paul entering a strange city and, by witnessing to first one and then another forming a Christian group, each member a vital witness. Here was the Book of Acts in action.

I opened my pulpit to this wonderful little man, this radiant Christian, and he spoke over the air to the Australian continent. The response was an avalanche of appeals—men and women in and out of the Church crying for what he had experienced. I gathered the ministers of all Churches together and turned Ivan Menzies loose upon us. Ministers were found confessing their own sins instead of one another's!

One perfect spring afternoon we two drove along the Bayside and talked our hearts out. This untheologically-minded, unusual evangelist began to probe me about the Group. Where did I stand in relation to it? I welcomed it—thanked God for it, at the same time being alive to its dangers. 'Are you absolutely surrendered to God?' he asked 'Yes,' I said, without any fencing, 'I can truthfully say that I have no ambition in this world but to do the will of God.' We were silent awhile. Then he asked, 'Do you absolutely surrender to God *every day*?' 'I have not consciously done so,' I confessed. Then he witnessed to what daily surrender had done for him. He begged me to check my life every day on the Four Absolutes

Love, Unselfishness, Honesty and Purity. He went on to ask about my work as a life changer. I told him how I had been constantly used in bringing men and women to Christ. 'That's grand,' he said, 'but are they life changers?' 'Well,' I replied, 'some of them are but I don't know about the others.' 'No one is really changed until he becomes a life changer,' he insisted, 'for that is the only way we can get God's plan working in the world.'

I saw it—I humbly and gratefully saw it all.

Much more we told each other. I went back to Melbourne committed to the Group, in it for all I was worth.

When I came to make a daily surrender I learned what a different experience this is from a general surrender. Daily checking on the four absolutes revealed to me things I had never questioned in myself. The Quiet Time was no new method of prayer to me but it became increasingly searching. I came to a daily willingness to do anything for God. I made amends where He gave me light. Now I know how the spiritual inertia of the Churches can be quickened. Now my world sickness has gone—I know how the world can be changed. Evil social and international conditions always are everywhere caused through individual evil lives. When individuals' lives are changed and brought together into groups—these groups are fellowships of reconciliation through which Christ can work.

Well, amazing things have happened in Melbourne. I have never seen anything like it in my life. At one of our recent house parties the witnesses to Christ were a minister, a society woman, a University student, a prisoner recently released from Pentridge, an insurance agent, a former Communist, a shop assistant and an architect. Some witnesses could not be present because they are still in gaol. Appropriately enough, they were represented by a young Melbourne solicitor who had been instrumental in changing some of them. Groups have sprung up everywhere and are penetrating the community far more vigorously than Communist cells. My office has become a soul clinic. Never a day passes but pagans and sub-Christians come asking how they can find a maximum experience of Christianity. My Church has become a dangerous place for those who want to be left alone, for anywhere the visitor may be challenged to an adventure with Christ. I am humbly grateful to have seen this day of God. The revival that we have been praying for is here—though some are still blinking at it. The great day of Christ is here. The trumpets are sounding across the world.

'Bliss was it in that dawn to be alive,
But to be young was very heaven!'

Appendix D

QUESTIONS AND ANSWERS

THE Group does not reply to criticisms. Lives that have been led to Christ by the Group witness are the positive answer. Questions are frequently asked at house parties and the following selection may prove of value:

Q. Is there anything new in the Oxford Group Movement?

A. It believes nothing that Christians of all creeds do not profess to believe. It teaches nothing that is not taught in the Gospels, the Book of Acts and the Epistles. It differs only in the uncompromising manner in which it translates the principles of the New Testament into everyday life.

Q. When people say that they belong to the Oxford Group, do they mean that they belong to Christ?

A. Most certainly they do. The Group is meaningless apart from Christ. The Oxford Group stands for a maximum experience of Jesus Christ.

Q. When the Group speak of God's direct guidance, how do they know that what they hear is really a message from God and not only a prompting of the sub-conscious mind? May not this guidance be misleading and dangerous?

A. It is possible to mistake the source of these impulses. But mistakes and dangers can be checked by applying a simple test to the guidance which we believe comes from God. He has given us the power to reason and compare. We are able to discern spiritual values, the higher from the lower, the Divine from the human. God makes Himself known to a surrendered life in the light of His will for the world and His plan for our lives. Guidance is tested by the Divine scale and standard of values.

Q. The Oxford Group appears to make salvation depend upon absolute surrender, whereas the New Testament puts the emphasis upon faith. Is this so?

A. Such a question is in danger of putting asunder what God has joined. How could anyone absolutely surrender to Christ unless he had faith in Him? The man who jumps from a burning aeroplane, trusting to his parachute, surrenders and trusts at the same time. So those who surrender to Christ have absolute faith in His power to make all things new in them.

Q. Does the Group forbid smoking, dancing, theatres, etc.?

A. The Group is not a revival of Pharisaism which adds the commandments of men to the commandments of God. What the Group insists upon is absolute surrender of everything to God—time, habits, pleasure included. Only those pleasures are fit which do not unfit.

Those who seek guidance as to what things are expedient may well ponder the counsel which Susannah Wesley wrote to her famous son, John, when he was at Oxford. ' Whatever weakens your reason, impairs the tenderness of your conscience, obscures your sense of God or takes off the relish of spiritual things—in short, whatever increases the strength and authority of your body over your mind, that thing is sin to you, however innocent it may be in itself.'

St. Paul uses very stern language about buffetting the body. Yet he is astonishingly liberal about rules of abstinence. 'He that eateth, eateth to the Lord, for he giveth God thanks; and he that eateth not, to the Lord he eateth not, and giveth God thanks. He that regardeth the day, regardeth it unto the Lord, and he that regardeth not the day, to the Lord he doth not regard it' (Rom. 14: 6). We may choose our own methods of self-denial, and the less public they are the better; so our Lord says in the Sermon on the Mount. But we must live in hard training. Each one must find, concerning each temptation, whether abstinence or temperance is the way of life for him.

Q. Is inability to observe the Quiet Time a bar to Group membership or spiritual growth?

A. Yes—definitely. No Christian can be vital without the Bible, prayer and guidance.

Q. Christianity has been tried and failed and therefore the Group message is out of date.

A. Let G. K. Chesterton answer that: 'Christianity has not been tried and found wanting; it has been found difficult and not tried.'

Q. How can one with no faith, without any real belief in God, come to know Christ?

A. See 'My Text' in this book.

M

Q. Do people who are changed by the Group stand?

A. No—they keep moving.

Cromwell wrote on the fly-leaf of his Bible: 'He who ceases to be better ceases to be good.' Those of the Group, like other Christians, fall backward when they fail to move forward.

Q. Must we confess all our faults to somebody?

A. When Dr. Buchman was, asked this very question he replied: ' Not necessarily. But everyone should be willing to do so if guided by the Holy Spirit.'

Q. Are the Groups critical of the Churches?

A. Dr. Buchman has replied to this question: ' Our business is not to criticize but to appreciate.' Those who belong to the Group are taught to live out that quality of life in their churchmanship as well as in their business.

Q. Is there any danger of the Oxford Group becoming a separate Church?

A. Not unless it is persecuted and driven out of the existing Churches, which may God forbid. Surely the Church will not repeat the tragic blunder of the eighteenth century and fail to recognize her children, leaving them to fend for themselves? This magnificent spiritual force ought to be incorporated in normal Church life. The matter rests very largely with the ministers. I am unwilling to believe that ministers will refuse sympathy and direction to men and women who have manifestly been ' changed,' thus leaving them to build their own spiritual lives as best they can. The

Groups cannot live without the discipline and the true sacramental life of the Church. Those in the Group are already in the Church or they are ready to enter it.

Q. I cannot see why it is necessary to confess one's sins to another person.

A. Confession as taught by the New Testament is two-way confession. 'Confess therefore your sins one to another that ye may be healed.' This is what the Group calls ' sharing.' It is not a matter of theory but a fact of experience that well-meaning but unhappy Christians have found victory by this practice. Sharing must be mutual so that both are helped. But such sharing is not a substitute for confession to God who alone can forgive.

If you are a Christian living victoriously over every known sin would you not be willing, if guided, to tell some poor struggler how Christ gave you power over a particular sin? If you are not living victoriously, try sharing. Sharing brings men and women face to face with Christ.

Q. Does not the popularity of the Oxford Group Movement make one suspicious that it is not of God?

A. What a question! Have you ever considered the extraordinary popularity of Jesus Christ and what a cause of offence that was to the Pharisees? It is not generally understood what an amazing success Jesus experienced among ' His own.' Hundreds and thousands in Galilee were influenced by Him, believed in Him and loved Him dearly. It was this very popularity that helped to stir up the priestly class against Him. They were annoyed at His success and jealous of Him. 'Woe unto you when all men speak well of you.' The Oxford Group is in no danger of incurring this woe. There is plenty of misrepresentation and uninformed criticism of it.

Q. Don't you think it rather rude of a member of the Group to ask a clergyman if he has absolutely surrendered?

A. Not at all—so long as it is done with Christian courtesy. Every minister in the Group is profoundly thankful that he was challenged. A. J. Russell says in *Christ Comes to Town*: 'Take no one for granted whether bishop or infidel. All must be freed from fear and ambition and be brought under the direction of the Holy Spirit.' Good ministers must become maximum ministers.

Q. Is not the Oxford Group's appeal largely in the promise of joy?

A. Joy is a product of the Holy Spirit (Galatians 5: 22, 23). Remember the saying of Hermas: 'The Holy Spirit is an hilarious Spirit.' Christianity is a religion of joy. No religious teacher ever spoke so much about joy as Jesus. It radiated from Him: 'My joy'—'I am come that your joy might be full.'

This question reminds me of two neighbours, one of whom asked the other: 'Was that the minister going down your steps just now laughing?' 'Yes, Mrs. Sanders,' came the answer. 'Religion isn't what it used to be,' observed the first neighbour. For that we may be very thankful.

Q. Is the Group modernist?

A. It is just as modern as Jesus Christ who is 'the same yesterday, to-day and for ever.'   Its message is, as Canon Grenstead has said, 'the one Gospel breaking out in terms that the present generation can understand.'

Q. Why insist on the Quiet Time in the *morning*?

A. Because we need strength and guidance to realize God's plan for us in all the affairs of each day.

Q. Why is the Group necessary when the same ideals are preached in the Church?

A. Because those very 'ideals' as you call them must be taken to those who are outside the Church and never hear them preached.   The 'outsider' will become an 'insider' through personal witness to Christ.   Many of those who are in the Churches need to have their spiritual experiences re-vitalized.

Q. If the Group has no new doctrines why is it necessary?

A. Where have you been living?   Read any history of the post-war years.   Read the newspapers.   Are you content with things as they are? Here is the testimony of that great Anglican scholar, Canon H. B. Streeter:

'During the last two and a half years one has been affected by the world situation, and one has felt that the world situation has been one full of depression, full of despair.   There is a great deal of goodwill, but there is not goodwill to solve tremendous problems—war, class war, and the rest—and the men of good-will are losing heart. And I think, speaking broadly, the Christian Church has been losing heart. . . . I have learned a good deal, or at any rate something, of why it is that this movement seems to be able not merely to change some bad people into good, but also to give new heart and a new courage and a new sense of direction to those who are already men of goodwill.

'I have come to the conclusion that in an age of growing world despair I feel it to be my duty to associate myself with a movement which seems to have got on to the secret of giving people new hope, new courage, and of increasing their number and their power.'

Q. What is the difference between surrender as taught by the Groups and conversion as taught by the Church?

A. Absolute surrender to which the Group witnesses includes all that the New Testament means by converting. It is conversion with a definite programme of world changing through life changing. The Group is insistent that every Christian must be a life changer. The New Testament knows nothing of a self-contained conversion.

Q. Does the Oxford Group regard Jesus Christ as the Saviour who gives them the victory over sin to which they witness?

A. The Oxford Group is only a means of bringing men and women into vital relationship with

Jesus Christ. He is the only Saviour. No one in the Group ever changed anybody. All that he can do is to introduce people to Christ and commend Him by personal witness.

Q. What do the Groups believe about the Cross?

A. The answer must be in terms of the Church to which the individual Group member belongs. It is the responsibility of the Church to teach doctrine. The Group presents a changed life to the Church to ' be instructed and trained in the doctrines, privileges, and duties of the Christian religion.'

The Christian Church has never formulated a doctrine of the Atonement. Every conceivable interpretation can claim some high authority; there is no interpretation which can claim supremacy.

The theology of the Cross may divide; the experience of the Cross unites. It may be said that the experience common to all varieties of Church members within the Group is that the Christ of the Cross is the only Saviour. The Group, like the New Testament, knows no other.

Q. Is not the Oxford Group more of a moral than a spiritual Movement?

A. No. You can no more have morality without religion than you can have perfume without the flower. Without spiritual faith there cannot be a high and progressive morality. Faith and morals are bound together in a living union. A morality without faith is powerless.

On the other hand, religious experience must find ethical expression. Let anyone examine the published sermons of so great an evangelist as John Wesley and observe how many of them are concerned with morality. Samuel Chadwick used to tell of a poor woman, who, not long after her conversion in the Leeds Mission, set off for her class-meeting. All the money she had in the world was the penny which she intended for her class dues. She had a long way to go, and it was raining in torrents. She therefore deliberated as to whether she would be justified in taking the tram, and came to the conclusion that under the circumstances that would be the wiser course. In the class-meeting she spoke of the goodness of the Lord, and told of her experience that very evening. She recounted how, after due deliberation, she had decided to take the tram, and concluded triumphantly by saying: 'But the Lord was good to me. When I had to get out He arranged for the conductor to be on top, and so I still have the penny for the class!' A religious experience needs ethical education.

Q. What is the aim of the Oxford Group?

A. 'Our aim is to see Jesus Christ, working through the Church, the one and only answer to personal, social, racial, national and international problems, perils and miseries' (Dr. Frank Buchman).

To this may be added the testimony of the Archbishop of Canterbury when speaking to his Diocesan Conference: 'The Oxford Group is most certainly doing what the Church exists everywhere to do. It is changing human lives. . . .'

Q. Why do the Groups concentrate on the better classes?

A. Which are the ' better' classes? All sorts and conditions are in the Groups—lawyers, charladies, doctors, domestics, Communists and unemployed. There is only one class distinction and that is fundamental—the changed and the unchanged.

Q. Is not sharing liable to be a form of exhibitionism?

A. Yes, if it is not checked, but read 1 Thessalonians 2.

Q. What is a Group?

A. A Group is a company of people drawn into fellowship by a common desire for a richer experience of the Living Christ and of the Holy Spirit, and united in the common task of winning souls for the Kingdom of God.

Q. Does the Group give the Bible due prominence?

A. Yes. A woman went into a Melbourne bookshop recently and asked for the best book on the Oxford Group. The bookseller produced a copy of Moffatt's Translation of the Bible and said: ' This is the book they are all buying.'

In Oslo (Norway) after the arrival of the Group team, it was not possible to procure a single copy of the Scriptures.

Those in the Groups are taught the indispensable necessity of daily Bible reading and meditation.

Q. Is not daily self-examination likely to lead to an unhealthy introspection?

A. Self-examination is of no avail unless the sight of our condition drives us to Christ. We shall be like the Highlander who bought a barometer and complained that it did not improve the weather. Introspection only reveals the condition —the remedy is with Christ. When the sight of what we are distresses us we are then ready for the Gospel that there is forgiveness in Christ. For every 'once' we look into our own hearts let us look up twice to Christ.

Q. Is not the Movement wrong in its insistence upon a definite conversion that can be pinned down to some specified time and place rather than upon the slow building-up of the religious life on a completely unemotional basis?

A. Are you not confusing conversion with salvation? Conversion is turning—the turning of the soul to Christ. Everybody needs conversion. The conversion of the Wesleys was the conversion of two very religious men. Conversion, or what the Group calls 'life changing,' is the crisis when a man turns to Christ. That deep, initial experience cannot be skipped or slurred. Now while conversion is a crisis—salvation is a process. The Book of Acts (2: 47, R.V.) says: 'The Lord added to them day by day *those that were being saved.*' The tense is emphatically present. 'Those who are being saved' are those who are being healed of all the tempers, passions and disturbances that are destroying their lives. 'He who began a good work in you will perfect it until the day of Jesus Christ.' Conversion is a beginning, not a terminus. If we have converted—turned—changed, we need to ask ourselves whether our lives are ' being saved,'—growing in grace and in likeness to Jesus Christ.

Q. Does the Group regard absolute surrender as everything?

A. No. But absolute surrender is the beginning of everything.

Q. Are not many people living the Christian life to which the Group witnesses without being in the Group?

A. Yes. It is not that the Group is one method and that others have other methods. Either we are living the maximum experience of Christ or not.

Q. Why do you not sing hymns at house parties?

A. There is not the slightest reason why hymns should not be sung, if Groupers feel guided to do so. Whenever a team conducts a service in a church, hymns are invariably sung. But a house party is not a formal religious service. It is just what the name suggests—an informal party where religion is discussed with candour, frankness and naturalness. Men and women speak of what Christ has done and is doing for them.

Q. What would you say to those who regard those in the Group as cranks?

A. Cranks are little things that make revolutions.

A THANKSGIVING

It is inevitable that as the Oxford Group Movement continues to spread throughout the nations of the earth it will create a literature of its own in various lands. This is an Australian exposition and witness, born of the life and needs of the Group in Melbourne.

It is a pleasure to record my thanks to Mr. Joseph Hocking, B.A., who generously read the manuscript and corrected the proofs. I invited Groups to check this book and I am indebted to them for valuable suggestions. Among the Group friends who read the manuscript are: Messrs. Alan Moyle, Geoffrey Littleton, F. Oswald Barnett, and the Revs. L. M. Thompson, M.A., John Sayers and W. H. Holloway. The Rev. C. O. Lelean co-operated with the above-named in submitting questions asked at House Parties.

Brown, Prior, Anderson Pty. Ltd., 430 Little Bourke St., Melb., C.1.

CPSIA information can be obtained at www.ICGtesting.com
Printed in the USA
BVOW10s1202240714

360189BV00005B/212/P